Bill Melville

During twenty years in journalism Bill Melville covered a broad range of sports, everything from athletics to tennis and triathlon including those as diverse as curling, orienteering, and rowing. His material appeared in national and regional press across the country, papers in Europe and press agency output in Canada, Australia and New Zealand.

After retiring, he didn't miss the pressure of meeting deadlines, but he missed the excitement and pleasure of writing. Taking up book writing needed a different approach, but, he says, "It brought alive that old feeling of working with words and hopefully bringing them alive."

Year of the Perfect Run
– a Quest

Bill Melville

peakpublish

Peakpublish
An imprint of Peak Platform
New Bridge
Calver
Hope Valley
Derbyshire S32 3XT
First published by Peakpublish 2012

Printed in England

A CIP catalogue record for this book is available from the
British Library

ISBN: 978-1-907219-30-6
www.peakplatform.com

1

The year of the perfect run. That is what I had in mind. That would be my quest.

What is it they say? As men grow old they lose everything but their ambition.

Of course, perfection is not easily come by.

However, I believe that anyone, anyone who runs and runs often enough to make running second nature, can have a perfect run.

Is that heresy?

The average man in the average pub knows a perfect run when he sees it. Chances are he would say, "That big, black guy at the Olympics." Chances are too that he has Usain Bolt in mind, and the giant Jamaican on his 100m world record breaking outing at the Beijing Olympics, or again, at the 2009 World Athletics Championships. Impressive performances they were. "Poetry in motion" status was the claim of world wide press hyperbole that greeted his success.

Needless to say – I'm no Usain Bolt and maybe I should say I'm no sprinter.

I should really come clean and say I don't and rarely have run on the track, and while I raced the roads and cross-country for many years that is not where my quest for perfection will take me.

A ten miler on the roads was always, to my mind the perfect running distance. The average club runner could go out and race it pushing themselves, keeping up leg speed, attacking the hills, working hard towards the finish. It is a distance which puts them under pressure but never empties the tanks. Get up towards half marathon distance and you have to ration your output. Finishing still in running mode, rather than racing becomes the objective.

Achilles tendon problems finished my road running career many years ago, and cross-country, well that's a winter pastime. For reasons more historical than sensible, there is no summer cross-country. I can think of nothing better than a good "park" style cross-country run on a sunny summer's afternoon, but that is another story.

No - I am going for a perfect run but I'm going for it in orienteering.

That's the sport where the course is marked on the ground by a series of flagged control sites where you check in electronically with a time chip. How you get around is up to you. All you have to help you is a map showing where the controls are sited, and a compass to keep you running in the correct direction. So it is map, compass, legs and thinking. That's orienteering.

Without orienteering, my running career would be a long time dead. With it, I am into my fifth decade of enjoying the sport nature intended, and while I am undoubtedly running slower than in my heyday, I am running better than ever.

Let's start by setting the record straight. At top level, orienteering is a fast running, all terrain, long distance time trial sport. Winning at top level requires quick thinking, quick decision making, physical stamina, and running skill.

One World Championships winner says, "I train using all the technique exercises track and field athletes do."

It is tough. How tough? Running coaches these days are talking about chaos theory.

Sprinting one hundred metres on the track has nil chaos value. It is a straight sprint on a level surface.

Double the distance and negotiating the bend comes into play, introduces that little bit of uncertainty, an element of chaos. You have to plan your way round.

Up the distance again and going over 800m and 1500m things outside your control really begin to happen. Not only do you have to make your way round the track but other runners can get in your way, and tactics designed to keep control come into play; other tactics in pace and place have to be considered.

The situation changes from second to second so this is more chaotic.

Leave the track, get out on the roads and it is not just the opposition which makes for chaotic going, it is the environment – camber, potholes, kerb stones, corners, hills going up and hills going down.

Take to the country and the chaos value increases yet again with changes in terrain and underfoot vegetation to cope with at every stride.

Orienteering is country running at its most chaotic. Like cross-country you are running up hill and down, on the level, on paths, fields and park land. Then, often as not, you will run across marsh, through forest, on soft ground, rough ground, boulder fields, through trees and bushes, and - think well on this - all of that could be found in the first quarter mile on the way to the first control point. That is just the first leg with maybe fifteen or more control points and ten to fifteen kilometres still to go. This is orienteering. This is chaos "big time".

That's not all. That's just the macro level chaos. Look more closely. Forest running especially keeps throwing up change and problems: branches, fallen trees, thickets, holes, hummocks, tussocks, all of which force changes in direction, stride, foot placement and posture. This is micro level chaos.

It doesn't get more chaotic than that.

One top British orienteer said she'd take on Paula Radcliffe any day in a forest run, and beat her.

Her claim was never put to the test. Chances are Paula would not have taken up the challenge if it had been issued. Forest running looks far too dangerous to most track and road runners, and Paula has too much invested in her legs to put them at risk.

Orienteering is no place for so called "wimps". This is the sport for the real runner, the all rounder, out not just to put the opposition under test but to test themselves as well.

Even running like a deer through the woods isn't good enough if you are going in the wrong direction.

You have to use the map. That's one giant size drawback.

Maps put many people off. A road map is enough set their pulse racing let alone a detailed map of some stretch of "wilderness".

3

Maps too, mean you have got to think about what you are doing, concentrate. Some opt out with the excuse that all that is a bit "intellectual" if not even "geeky".

It doesn't appeal to everyone, and that means many people who fancy their brain power.

They don't mind being beaten at running, biking, swimming or paddling in a race and are willing to admit that they are not as fit or as strong or as technically perfect as the guy who crossed the line half a mile in front. They console themselves – or maybe fool themselves - by grumbling, "If I put in the bloody great mileages they do in training, I'd be up there with them, maybe beating them."

They are unwilling to admit that some other guy is a better, quicker thinker, might even have a better brain. Their self belief takes a battering as they refuse to recognise that the brain needs just as much training in map reading and the thinking that goes with it as their muscles do for running.

You have to keep a check on your location, picking off the hills, paths, marshes and so on along your chosen route. The best do that without slackening pace.

Your concentration suffers a three way split between running style, where you are, and where you want to be.

A perfect orienteering run, then, doesn't just mean perfect running, it needs perfect thinking, perfect control, perfect decision making as well, to "spike" every control spot on.

Orienteering has a poor image in some quarters: anorak and walking boots. Much of that idea dates way back to a school outing with a pack of other runny nosed primary kids wandering in the woods, or back to the occasional meandering hike with the local scout troop in the hills.

It is the sort of sport everybody thinks they might have done at some time but even if they have, few have done it well. They haven't tried it often enough or long enough and certainly were never skilled enough or fit enough to do it well.

Forget it.

Running on the track, the roads or the country can make you feel good. Pub philosophers are likely to say it is all the chemicals in the brain. The pain produces "endorphins" which, like a number of man made drugs, make you feel good. These are people who don't run; people who feel pain and break sweat if they up the tempo to a fast walk down the boozer, let alone try to run there.

They are not fit enough to understand or if they are it is because they have gained their fitness in other ways and not with running.

Running can hurt, especially at the end of a long outing when the muscles are both running out of energy and are suffering the combined effects of repeated contractions and absorbing the impact.

Runners know that once you get into your rhythm, there is no pain. Brain chemicals might be making you feel good - brain chemicals are responsible for most of your feelings and thinking - but they are not there because the runner is feeling pain. It has all to do with limb speed and movement.

Most of my working life I was a sports journalist. In an interview with Olympic cyclist Chris Boardman some years ago he let drop that there was a magic leg pace which saw the legs not only working at their most efficient but with minimal effort. That turn over pace was around ninety revolutions per minute. This struck a chord for I had already noticed the same magic number applied in running – ninety double strides or 180 total leg movements.

Hitting the magic number in leg pace combined with the optimum level of exertion, or muscle output, carries maximum dividends in the "feel good" factor. You may not be running as fast as the winner, but out there you can feel just as good as they do.

So, a first class road, track, trail or country run makes you feel good.

A first class orienteering run makes you feel good too.

Add the navigation element and you don't just feel good, you feel good and then some, like reading a really good book while you are having a really good run.

Someone once said that running is better than sex. If that's so, said another wag, then orienteering is better than sex with the Kamasutra.

In this case, of course, it isn't an instruction manual you are reading, it is a map.

Mapping is a work of art. The mapper is out to translate the world around him into a picture. Three dimensions become two with contours used to show the ups and downs and the subtle shapes and land forms. Paths and fences become black lines, streams, lakes and marshes are drawn in blue. Boulders, crags, cairns, benches, statues, houses all have their symbols. If it is out there it is on the map... well, usually it is on the map.

The art of the mapper is to simplify the area. In really complex terrain a small hill on the map may turn out to look like a fistful of knuckles on the ground. If there are too many boulders to make sense of, only the big ones will be mapped.

Beginners find map colours confusing. Since most O-events are held in woodland, runnable forest is mapped in white. Green shows that the woods there are thicker, more difficult to run through and see through. Impassable areas or thickets will be marked in very dark green and so on down to light green, a stretch with a few young trees that will slow you down but not by much. Open areas are various shades of brown depending on whether it is rough or easy going.

The orienteer has to translate the map into the world around them.

Nowhere else does art demand such a close relationship between the artist and his public, for their success or failure depends on how closely they can connect with the mapper's "masterpiece."

It is up to the runner to convert what they see around them into what they see on the map, and at the same time match up what they see on the map into what they see around them.

It's a bit like a guide book. It is telling you where to run and what to watch out for. While the guide book tells you one particular way through a stretch of country, there is no end to the ways a map can show the way to go.

It is up to you to pick your own route, the way that suits you best, and at the same time the pressure is on to do it all at speed.

So? .....well, a good orienteering run gives you all the physical excitement of any other good run.

Running off road brings extra rhythm – not an extra stride but an extra beat on the high hat. It makes it more lively. Running off road and off path on ground as nature intended, has you running as nature intended. It has a euphoria that is hard to beat.

Using the map on the run brings a mental elation, each feature ticked off carries it own little burst of stimulation, like the surge of mental relaxation that comes with solving a crossword clue, or the great feeling the golfer experiences when he whacks the ball far down the fairway.

Topping a rise to the control kite where you expect it to be, in a depression, at the foot of a crag or beside a boulder rings up its own special feeling of success, akin to the golfer's "high" when he sinks the ball into a hole.

It's like a game of tennis where each centre of the racquet strike gives that same thrill, but if you can play your opponent around the court and then play the winner you've worked for it is so much better.

Orienteering can feel just that exciting.

Let's forget that for the moment; let's go back to the beginning. Let's just think about some of the perfect runs and perfect runners, some of the legends of running history.

If sprint enthusiasts go for Bolt or nine times Olympic gold winner Carl Lewis, middle distance aficionados – and I am one of these – might well argue the point suggesting Britain's Seb Coe and Steve Ovett, who set world tracks on fire with their 800m and 1500m outings in the 1980s, were and still are rivals for any crown for perfection that might be going.

Just for starters, the 800m must be the most perfect of all track races.

The fast staggered start, the jockeying for position at the break, a brief settling of the status quo round the bottom bend before heading for the bell with half an eye watching out for any breaks or drives from behind.

Then it is into the second lap with the field, sometimes strung out, sometimes bunched, everyone straddling a metaphorical line between perfection and going over the top, with anyone liable to make a telling move down the back straight or going into the final bend before making a final sprint for the line.

Early in my sports journalist career, I spent much time covering events other journalists did not touch. I was getting to know the business, establishing my credentials. I could make money that way.

7

I can remember a night of 800m finals at one of the early World Masters Track Championships in Verona. Men and women from forty to over ninety raced for their age group titles. The younger ones probably carried a pound or two more than they did at their best, older legs looked stringier, skin hung looser, limbs and backs were not as straight as they once had been but they ran with style. Without exception, the best of them produced that easy, rhythmic, "feel good" action that even the most inexperienced spectator must appreciate and enjoy.

Somewhere in your genes there must be a chemical pattern which helps you appreciate the beauty of a flawless runner in action. It's like looking at a fine picture.

There is something primitive about it, maybe something that goes back to distant days when running meant the difference between eating and going hungry, death or survival, something that all but the artistically inept must appreciate.

Any runner could see that they had that "flying feeling" as they glided along without effort and with no hint of exhaustion.

Without enough time and distance for the competitors to run out of strength and stamina, "run out of legs", each race was full of tension and uncertainty as well as a thrill to watch and, hopefully, thrilling to run.

So there were two hours of superlative athletics entertainment, without a current world top ten runner amongst them.

The perfect run is no easy find for the best in the world if for no other reason than that their superlative abilities set the bar at a higher level. Running and racing closer to the edge it is easier for them to slip off.

Coe and Ovett were masters at the art of 800m running, both able to lead from the start or come from behind over the final 200m with remarkable speed and acceleration but with an ease which took them over the line scarcely breathing deeply, untroubled by their efforts.

They met up but rarely, but their rivalry, as first one and then the other would break a middle distance record, sparked world level running for more than a decade.

8

I have always said Ovett was the better runner. During his illustrious athletics career he ran with success at national level over a whole gamut of distances from 400m on the track to the half marathon on the roads.

His international career over he set up a runners' holiday business in Scotland and while building up his new career in television - he worked as a commentator with International Athletics productions - he kept his running ticking over, training regularly. He dabbled in triathlon and ran regularly for the Annan club in cross-country where he was unbeatable by the best of the Scots runners at that time.

Of the two, Ovett was arguably the better all-rounder, but equally arguably, Coe was the more poetic mover, had the smoother action, ran with more appreciable perfection.

Athletics fans still argue the point.

Did their dramatic wins and record breaking outings come from perfect runs?

Former world 5000m record holder Dave Moorcroft has said that he had a perfect run on that historic night in 1982 when he set alight the Bislett Stadium in Oslo. During its long history, Bislett has enjoyed the reputation of producing the most exciting night of non-championship athletics of the year. The crowd and the athletes are "on fire" producing that electric atmosphere on which competitors thrive and come up with world class, if not world record breaking, performances. There are many world marks in the Bislett history book.

The men's 10000m world record was broken no fewer than four times at Bislett before the turn of the millennium, starting with the great Australian Ron Clarke in 1965. Clarke, who in 1965 broke eleven world records over a period of six weeks, became renowned as the best distance runner never to win a major championship medal.

I saw his farewell appearance at London's White City Stadium when he jogged round the track waving to the crowd at six minute mile pace.

The Bislett Dream Mile, arguably the major event at the meeting each year, saw the world record broken twice first by Ovett in 1980 and then by Steve Cram in 1985.

The women's hall of record breaking fame includes local Norwegian greats Greta Waitz and Ingrid Kristiansen, both of whom won the London and New York marathons.

On Moorcroft's night of nights at Bislett he ran away from the field, leading Kenya's then world record holder Henry Rono by over a hundred metres with two laps to go.

Speaking on an excellent BBC distance running DVD, Moorcroft says of that night, "I was in the best condition I'd ever been in. I was running really well and had done 3m49s for the mile in Oslo a couple of weeks before."

He explains, "Every runner can probably count on the fingers of one hand the number of times they race and it has been perfect."

The perfect run. What is it like?

"You just feel so light," says Moorcroft. "You feel you can run faster. You don't feel any pain."

He says of that record breaking run, "It was fast, and for ten or eleven laps I was just completely flowing, the most relaxed and in control that I'd ever been. I was running faster than I had ever done before."

Moorcroft's track career was dogged by injury both before and after his world record breaking win. He had been operated on for a calf injury at the end of the previous season. He retired aged thirty-one in 1984. However, on that night in Norway he had run a time which stood as a world mark for five years and survived as the British record until 2010.

Of course people, have since run 5000m faster than Moorcroft, the 800m faster than Coe. Sprinters, including Bolt, have run much faster than 1938 Olympic Champion Jesse Owens, but that does not mean that Moorcroft, Coe and Owens did not have perfect runs.

Owens, by the way, enjoyed not just a perfect run but a perfect afternoon at a meet in Ann Arbor, Michigan in 1935, when he equalled the world 100 yard record with 9.4s, broke the 220 yard mark with 20.3s and the 220 yard hurdles time with 22.6s. His world long jump record that afternoon, taped at 8.13m, stood for twenty-five years.

In the 1936 Olympics he won four gold medals including those for the 100m and 200m.

Much political capital has been made of Hitler supposedly snubbing the black athlete.

Owens, who, in Berlin, found himself allowed to stay at the same hotel as his white team mates for the first time, reportedly dismissed such claims, saying that it was the US president who snubbed him. It rankled that he did not get a congratulatory telegram and was never invited to the White House.

He did get a ticker tape welcome in New York, however, but afterwards on his way to the reception in his honour at a major Manhattan hotel, the story goes, he was not allowed to use the lift that white folks used to reach the reception room. He was told to use the freight elevator.

Moorcroft, despite his perfect run, is not the world's all-time fastest at 5000m. So while he topped the world rankings back in 1982, he is not topping the world rankings today, but he still had his perfect run.

Equally well, the best women in the world do not run as fast as the best men but that does not mean that a woman can never have a perfect run.

So a perfect run does not have to be the best or even eye-catchingly fast.

Your perfect run is probably the best you can do with the equipment you have, in short, the body you have and the state it is in.

Indeed, most runners in athletics, triathlon and orienteering will remember those times when they are running better than clockwork.

They can read Moorcroft's description of his perfect run at Bislett and think, "I know what he means. I have felt just like that." It may have been during a training run. It may have been at a race or other event. It may have lasted only five minutes or ten. It could have lasted an hour or more. They may have done it only once. They may get that feeling every time they put on their running shoes.

Most find that keeping that perfect run feeling for the whole race or event hard to come by, and such outings, as Moorcroft says, are rare, but anyone can have a perfect run. It is no heresy to say so.

2

So suddenly, almost surprisingly, as if it didn't happen every year, it was into January in what I planned to be my Year of the Perfect Run.

The clock was ticking.

My thinking was that it could come early, maybe my first time out. If it did, then the quest would continue chalking up each time I did it, making perfection and consistency the rule rather than an occasional sporting artefact.

However, it might take a little longer. I realised that. In fact, if experience was anything to go by it would take a lot longer. My history in the sport told me that. All those years in orienteering and I couldn't remember one perfect run.

Successful orienteers are the height of cool. Under pressure they keep their cool. When the chips are down they stay with it. When things go wrong they don't lose the plot. They have their plan and a proven technique and they keep to both of them. It's all to do with mental approach rather than mental ability or cleverness.

On the other hand, I'm a seat of the pants competitor. Making decisions quickly, often too quickly, changing my mind, switching routes midway, often going for the fun option – a run through a tempting stretch of open, sunny woodland - rather than keeping to the plan.

So if my quest was a serious bid for perfection I knew that I would have to ditch running on impulse and take up running by blueprint, and I knew that that would be difficult, I knew that I was my own biggest obstacle to obtaining that success.

In any case, it was time to get ready, plan the month ahead and up the training.

January is the month to recover from Christmas.

Despite good intentions, Christmas always means too much wine, beer, food; too many Christmas calories. The trouble is it all tastes too scrumptious: turkey and trimmings; I'm a glutton for roast potatoes and stuffing; Christmas pud, mince pies, Christmas cake, all that traditional stuff including chocolates with after dinner coffee.

It is a problem for any runner, especially if festivities eat into their training time.

Eating more than ordinary seems to effect little change at first but then – usually around the day after the day after Christmas Day – there comes an explosion in weight.

In my case, as with any other runner, that might mean three or four extra pounds.

One big eat I can handle. A couple of runs, a mile or two on Christmas morning and another outing the following day along with a cut in intake keeps my weight in check.

With the family around for several days, plus the social outings with friends and neighbours, the two and even three course feeding extravaganzas become almost run of the mill; it is more or less impossible to run far enough and often enough to use up that extra energy consumption.

Weight makes a big difference to a runner.

Knowing this has enticed a number of sports people into eating disorders like anorexia. They get sucked in to thinking that they are never light enough and that discarding a pound or so more will take them closer to international success. It sometimes does. A number of top flight women runners have had so little body fat that they have lost their menstrual cycle. It seems that the body opts out of the risk of pregnancy if there is too little by way of energy reserves to support the developing child.

Sometimes there is pressure on big time hopefuls to lose weight.

A cyclist who was knocking at the door of international selection and in her national squad walked away when she found that their training "camp" involved long pre-breakfast squad outings designed primarily to knock off the pounds. She was not prepared to take the risk that shrugging off the pounds might become an addiction.

My running weight is nine and a half stone, that's a few points over sixty kilos. It is years since I last tipped the scales at that but it remains my objective.

At that weight I feel right, I feel so terrific floating along with a spring in my step - what I like to call a wolf-like spring. Some years ago, on a visit to a zoo I was amazed by the sight of a pack of wolves on the move in their large enclosure.

I don't believe in zoos, their ethos, the way the animals are confined, despite the now well established managerial drive to supply both adequate habitat space and the chance to enjoy normal behaviour.

No fenced space can make up for the loss of mixing with their own kind and with other species in the great outdoors. On the other hand, some, and by that I mean some of them, the animals, might argue that square meals more or less on demand and freedom from predator danger is more than adequate compensation.

At any rate, long ago during my teaching days, I decided that it was making best use of what I saw as just one step removed from cruelty to animals if they could help the next generation of human kind gain an appreciation of their fellow earthlings. So I took classes to the zoo and they went round armed with worksheets and pencils and packed lunches.

On one such day, passing the wolf enclosure my attention was drawn to the three or four light grey, light weight European wolves housed there. They were on the move, not running but trotting across the skyline of a small hill.

These long distance running hunters were so light on their feet, moving with such ease, for all the world as if they were on springs or blessed with a miniature trampoline in each leg. They didn't bounce. They glided, apparently, if impossibly, above the ground.

The runner in me was transfixed. Just for a few moments nothing else existed. It was a joy to behold and a lesson worth the learning.   Ever since, I've kept it in mind. More importantly, whenever possible, I have tried to keep it in my legs and running, the more so when the overall going is tough and I'm looking for a way back to running nirvana.

One thing for sure, there was no weight problem for them.

I look on ten stone, (60.5 kilos) as my upper limit for running. Pass that and I'm heading for trouble, carrying the equivalent of one or two bags of sugar with every stride. The alternatives are slow down and lose rhythm or maintain pace at terrible expense. Rapidly tiring legs become anaerobic leaving you gasping for breath.

At this stage I usually stop to recover. If orienteering I walk, using the time to check out my map.

I prefer recovery stops to the alternative of running on ever slower until all the fun has been squeezed from the outing, leaving it, like my legs, as empty as a squashed orange. My training sessions are often a mixture of fartlek – speed play – and interval running, both particularly excellent approaches to training for my particular sport.

Orienteering is a bit like that for all but the very best – a series of runs punctuated by brief stops or periods of slow running as you pass through a control site, relocate, or explore the map to plan the next section of the course.

I suppose on a really perfect run, while I might slow down to spike the controls I would not stop.

I have an additional danger that comes with overeating. From time to time and in certain situations, the extra spare tyre of abdominal fat which comes with these extra pounds presses on my heart bringing on a bout of palpitations - cardiac arrhythmia - forcing me to up my beta blocker dosage.

One of the revelations that comes with being an ageing runner is the number of exercise "decrepits" you meet out there who use beta blockers or some other pharmaceutical device to control heart rate problems. The problem with beta blockers is that they slow the heartbeat, reduce the energy supply to the muscles, increase recovery time; in short, slow you down.

So come Christmas, my usual plan involves a festive build up in training, ignoring the temptations to slacken off and join in the fun, I keep the training sessions to a maximum and keep the weight to a minimum. Then comes a week of binge eating and drinking which takes in the Christmas and New Year celebrations. That behind me, January is the month to burn off the inevitable fat built up and get the weight back down to a normal sub-ten stone level.

However, this year, the snow came.

A white Christmas is an oddity, isn't it? Bookies welcome bets on it hoping to make a killing. However, the week before

Christmas much of the country awoke to a snow bonanza. Would it last? Four inches fell overnight in our Dunkeld stretch of the Tay Valley, festooning the trees and giving the houses in the village that Christmas card look.

Around eleven I went for a run wearing trousers, gloves and hat, the cold air biting at my face and making my eyes nip. I covered somewhere around four miles, worth five in the conditions.

This bit of country is nature's gift to the off road runner with mile after mile of forest track and cross country terrain. I went up through the giant firs around the Hermitage trail (one, a Douglas fir, was credited with being the tallest tree in Britain for many years) before crossing the valley at the ancient stone bridge just below Braan Falls.

Here, water cascades over three giant buttresses and plunges into a pool ten feet or so below before dashing off through a gully and under the bridge to a big fish pool just beyond.

At its most spectacular, but not at its most picturesque, I have seen the torrent fill the drop and almost fill the gorge.

From time to time, salmon, intent on reaching upper river breeding grounds, can be seen braving the jump up the falls. Some people say that some fish make it, in two or three stages, but most can be seen falling back into the cauldron of foam below. As a last resort they will breed in the gravel fringes of the "big pool".

I have seen an otter here too. As I paused in my run one day to take in the view of the falls, a sleek brown, streamlined body surfaced just beneath the bridge, turned and dived again without stopping.

At twilight, Daubenton bats feeding on insects flying above the water dash this way and that, wheeling just above the pool below the bridge.

In the cold that morning, the falls were covered in ice and icicles but they were still carrying an impressive display of water.

A minor landslip had taken out a short stretch of the high riverside path beyond, but after carefully negotiating it I headed for home.

The going was good, soft and not too slippery, but I knew that would not last. Inevitably, the more people who walked the path in what is a popular walking area, the more icy and rough underfoot it would become and running would become really difficult. I was getting the best of it.

I put in another workout when I got home, shovelling snow from the garden path, for that very same reason. It would become treacherous with use and a fall within a few metres of the door would be hard to take.

The next morning we woke to find another ten inches of snow on the ground and another three fell through the day. This was "once in a generation" stuff.

View from my window - to run or not to run,
that is the question (Katherine Melville)

Running was really tough with high knees needed to clear the snow and with little traction underfoot.

It was also cold with day temperatures sinking to minus six or seven degrees centigrade.

Scotland has a reputation for being both cold and wet but these things are all relative and freezing conditions like these are a rarity. The fact that they were to continue into March

17

with snow in the mountains lasting until May made it doubly if not quadruply so.

The Scottish skiing industry has been in the doldrums for some twenty years. In the early eighties, the weekend outing to the slopes at Aviemore and the Lecht, near Aberdeen, became the done thing for the city "yuppies", the cars speeding up and down the A9 with skis strapped to the roof rack. Some flew north from London and the like.

The Aonach Mor slopes were opened within sight of Ben Nevis, with a grand new gondola lift.

Then it all ground to a virtual stop with limited snow falls year after year, and what fall there was melting too soon thereafter.

This winter would reverse the trend, but despite reports of sizeable turn outs it could take several more similar winters to re establish the habit.

In those early weeks, I kept running as much as possible even making rare outings on the road through the village which was well cleared and salted.

Our riverside run covered with patchy ice beneath the snow, was not so much rough as bevelled and really hard on the ankles.

I pulled my VJ Scandinavian orienteering shoes from the cupboard and geared up with O-leggings to keep my track trousers and long-johns dry.

The shoes have rubbers studs and even more crucially, small metal pegs or dobbs sticking out of these.

They are designed for running on ice and while the "skite" factor is still there, you can run with them on and do so with little danger of a dangerous fall.

The family arriving for Christmas provided some company out on the trails and the incentive to get out there.

We have a small running club in Birnam which attracts people from other villages round about. Most are other orienteers. Some are hill runners. Some don't compete at all. They just enjoy getting out to run. It meets Thursday nights to take in one or other of the forest or river circuits around the village and carries on for most of the winter using head torches.

Our Christmas Eve outing on the Thursday afternoon was a climb on Birnam Hill – some of us walking, others, the better of the hill competitors, running. The steep climb on the slope overlooking the village is more dangerous on the descent than on the climb, so after tea and mince-pies on the summit, we went the long, easy way home ploughing through thigh deep snow in places.

Just in case you are wondering, this Birnam is Shakespeare's Birnam mentioned in his less than true play, Macbeth. A massive oak by the river's side is claimed as the last of the Birnam Wood that supposedly disguised the troops attacking Dunsinane castle. Dunsinane Hill - pronounced dunsinan – is one of the Sidlaw range, about twelve miles away as the crow flies. The summit is covered in earth works carried out by amateur archaeologists searching for the remains of Macbeth's mythical castle

We kept the sessions going with path clearing, walking and more very tough running.

The snow brought down a tree next the Hermitage path landslip blocking the way completely, so we had to expand the circuit into the forest and take a longer way home.

We went sledging.

There is a first-rate "nursery" slope in the park area opposite our house and a fifty metre plunging descent on the golf course which I tried for the first time. It was fast, almost too fast, and bouncy!

Was it cold! Bitterly so. Ploughing to a stop into the soft snow at the bottom sprayed a shower of icy snow crystals onto your face.

It was all great fun, as the season should be.

I was looking forward to our family trip to Sidmouth in Devon in January for what I was already calling a "warm weather training stay", planning to get some serious miles under my ever expanding belt.

However, horror of horrors, the day before we left it snowed there too. The car thermometer was reading minus nine as we headed down the final drop on the M5 towards the south coast.

I had been looking forward to an orienteering event at Hor Tor to get my season underway but it was cancelled.

Sidmouth was a fishing village until the early nineteenth century when hotels like the Bedford were built to meet the new aristocratic holiday demand. The demand expanded over the next two hundred years but the town has kept its charm with a clutter of small streets with interesting shops and pubs nestling behind a promenade lined with Georgian styled hotels and houses boasting fine ironwork balconies. It is framed by cliffs in various shades of red and white which rise and dip steeply off towards Exmouth to the West and Lyme Regis to the East.

It is a London retirement suburb with a plethora of comfortable looking houses which are home to former city executives who dressed in beige wander along behind their spouses on shopping trips, a distant almost dreamy look in their eyes.

Some of the higher cliff tops are backed by a mixture of moorland and plantation – vintage running ground. While the snow in Sidmouth was thin, it was thicker on the more exposed heights and that, along with the cold, made training there out of the question.

There are sheltered parks in the town including a stretch along the River Sid and these gave scope for daily outings, a slow out and back, or hill and rough ground intervals.

Our week almost over, the thaw came just before we left and I managed a jog up Salcombe Hill and a pleasant woodland run at the top. I attacked the final climb from the town on my way home and kept the rhythm going all the way to the top. It felt easy and very satisfying.

Back in Scotland too, the thaw was underway but it would be another two weeks of slushy, icy going on the trails before they would be runnable. Worse still, it was more than a six weeks since I had been out in terrain with a map.

I had been toying with the idea of going to Portugal where the spring season gets underway in February with a couple of international events which usually attract a big entry from northern Europe. Without the background terrain training this was out of the question. I could not justify the expense.

So the year of the perfect run got off to a less than perfect start. I was overweight and under trained.

It was with some doubt if not trepidation that after weighing up the odds I submitted an entry for the first national event of the season near Sheffield at the end of January - the north of England Championship

3

Orienteering is a reflection of life. Often it shows up the ways we react to problems in work, in relationships and just living in general. Top of the list is the way we jump to conclusions. The brain is a great computer. It can't chalk up as many complex mathematical computations per minute as the average man made, electronic computer but it is the superior machine when it comes to taking in and processing information. It is superior because it can generalise – jump to conclusions.

It doesn't take a rocket science brain to understand that there are times when jumping to a right conclusion could prove life saving. If you have to see the tiger before you start running away then you aren't going to make it. A noise in the undergrowth in tiger country should be all that's needed. If you are wrong – so what, you live on.

The trouble is that jumping to conclusions is what people do even when there are no tiger-sized dangers around.

So it is in orienteering. Some people avoid jumping to conclusions at any cost Under pressure, they like to play safe, take time to weigh up all the information on the map and on the ground around them ticking off each spur, stream and marsh. However, they don't win. They spend too much time thinking about things that don't matter. They don't even have an enjoyable run.

At the other end of the spectrum are the vast majority of competitors who, under pressure and with a thirst to do well if not win, jump to too many conclusions, failing to check them out against the wealth of information available.

They don't win either. They make too many mistakes, at worst spending too much time running like a headless chicken in the wrong places notching up one blunder after another.

The winners are the ones who take the time to take in the minimum of information needed to jump to the correct conclusion.

Thierry Gueorgiou, the French runner who won seven world and three European titles by the time he was thirty, adopts a technique geared to wiping out just that fault making the most of running fast while navigating superbly well.

Like many high class runners he does not know why he is fast.

"Most of the time it is an unconscious process," he says. "My focus is on maintaining good balance and I think a lot about using my arms."

With speed and accuracy his hallmark, it is no surprise that nine of his ten gold medals were won in middle distance orienteering while the other came from a sprint.

With both parents PE teachers involved in orienteering, the young Thierry was always likely to be an orienteer even if not a champion.

He started when he was five and went on to be one of France's top juniors gaining his first international team place at the European Youth Championships in the mid 1990s and won gold at two championships in a row before going on to take silver and bronze at Junior World Championship level.

France did not have any great reputation in orienteering at that time so nobody really expected a great deal more from him but he did.

British orienteers were knocking loudly at the door of international success at this period. Yvette Baker won short course gold at the 1999 World Championships.

Some of them would laugh slyly up there sleeves at the French.

They don't now. Gueorgiou stopped that.

Into the early years of the new millennium nobody but Gueorgiou took notice when his first senior world outings met with relative failure.

Of course that was to be expected when he had just moved up from the ranks of the juniors. Very few orienteers, especially amongst the men, break through to the top in their early twenties. It is a sport where maturity, plus the control and strength that come with it, plays an important role at world level.

After finishing down in eighteenth place in the 2001 World Short Distance Championship in Finland, despite spending much of the year training on the notoriously difficult Finnish terrain, he realised something was wrong.

Apart from producing many top calibre competitors, Finland is noted for two things in orienteering, its trackless, marshy forests where everything looks very much the same, and the rough often stony running.

The French man was not going to accept excuses like that.

He realised that he had to go faster and set about analysing his technique to see how he could improve it.

Gueorgiou once told reporter, Jan Stricka, "At that time I always knew where I was in the forest. I was reading off features as I passed them so I was not even running in the present. I was running in the past.

I realised what was needed was to know where I am going.

Now I may be running through a certain bit of space but in my mind I am already some two hundred metres ahead."

He runs with a picture of where he is going in his head.

Not interested in where he is, he is looking far ahead.

"I keep my head up and look for features as distant as possible and run as fast as I can to them."

He doesn't mean any old feature. He means one on the map leading from his current position to the next control – landmark features.

He is ignoring the terrain in between these landmark features.

"Of course it is a much more challenging way to orienteer," he reminds.

"Many young orienteers run the way I did back then. It is the natural way and of course, you have to work really hard to change."

Gueorgiou benefits from first class translation abilities, picturing the land he sees on the map so that he can pick a corridor to run along and pick out these landmarks.

Like all top orienteers, he simplifies the map and the terrain, limiting the amount of information he is taking in but taking in enough to reach the correct conclusion.

This, he says, has developed over his many years in competition starting when a seven year old.

"Visualising is of the highest importance to me," he says. "If you don't know where you are going, you will probably end up somewhere else."

He says, demonstrating the level to which he has taken this skill, "I always believe that when you stand on the start line you should feel like you are about to run in your back garden."

Visualisation, Gueorgiou points out, depends on building up a brain data bank of information based on running through terrain map in hand, taking in detail from both.

Feeding the brain computer quickly and accurately relies on first class vision.

Eyes are as important as legs to an orienteer.

That's one of the major differences between orienteering and other running sports. While the eyes are important in all of them, orienteering with its highly chaotic content uses distance, middle distance and close vision in equal amounts.

Picking your way over rough terrain at speed, map reading and finding control sites put a heavy premium on the need for sharp all round sight.

Reading the map, reading it on the run if possible, is not an option, it is an essential.

I have long held that world class orienteers have exceptional vision. They don't just have twenty twenty vision, they have a superior depth of vision which takes in and mentally processes their surroundings, and they have the visual skill to filter the wealth of information on the map - contour shapes, line features point features and all the colours, at a glance.

I can remember one British internationalist reporting how she had picked up a small path through some dense vegetation, on her route between a couple of controls. It had given her maybe twenty-seconds or even half a minute advantage over the alternative detour. She had picked it up on the move and under pressure of competition. I could see it on the map, but not right away and only with difficulty.

Some people have inferior vision from the outset. That would include me. I have worn glasses and suffered from short sight since my late teens.

Most others develop it with the advancing years. Into your forties, usually around 45, the first signs of ageing begin to affect vision.

Try reading the phone book in artificial light. If you have difficulty reading an address or a number then that is a sure sign your vision in decline.

If you pick up the latest electronic gizmo and read the instructions and you need to get out the magnifying glass then the same thing goes.

Little wonder older people begin to feel excluded from the fast moving world of electronic digital gadgets. All the info on screen as well as off is printed in youth size type giving those with ageing eyes little chance of using it quickly and building up an expertise. After working their way through the intricacies of one machine with one metaphorical hand tied behind their back another one comes on the market and they are back to square one.

They become the laughing stock, the subject of snide, taunting remarks about their brain power.

Disability laws do a lot for those with mobility problems but do little for those with visual problems of whatever age and for whatever reason.

Sight begins to go because the lens and the ligaments suspending it begin to lose their elasticity so the ability to change focus begins to go too.

Then floaters – tiny, floating, black threads of eye debris - begin to get in the way of seeing clearly. Finally the acuity, the ability to see small spots of detail in focus or otherwise, begins to deteriorate. It is not unusual for the lens to toughen and lose its transparency as cataracts develop.

With or without cataracts, the eye needs reasonably high levels of light to see properly. Reading in artificial light or, in the case of the orienteer, in the dark of a forest, becomes very difficult.

Some orienteers have defective vision from an early age.

The short sighted will have no problem with map reading but most will have worn distance glasses for years.

Many years ago, before my reading vision deteriorated, I decided that narrow-lensed distance glasses were my way around my vision problem – I would look through them into

25

the distance and under them when reading the map. I approached one of the high street opticians.

They took a deal of convincing.

"We could make bifocals," they said.

"I can read OK. I only need them to see in the distance. I want to be able to look below the lenses for reading."

"We could make them bifocals with plain glass in the lower half," they responded.

"Looking through any glass makes seeing less clear," I argued.

So they agreed to give it a go.

The first attempt went adrift as the technician centred the curvature in the centre of one lens while the other was centred as if it was a "whole" lens cut in half.

I went off only to return half an hour later feeling slightly seasick and with a headache looming.

A second attempt gave me what I wanted.

Narrow, horizontal frame glasses later became very fashionable but I don't imagine that I started the craze.

One problem with distance glasses is that they tend to flatten out the field of view, reduce the three dimensional image produced by your brain from the two slightly different pictures seen by each of your eyes. The shapes of the land become less distinct and distance judgement less sure.

Being long sighted is even more of major drawback. You can see the land and markers no bother at all but reading the map, I could say, the all important map, is a problem. Reading glasses are a necessity.

Many fortunate people have top class reading and long distance vision throughout their early adult years.

So, it is not until they are in their mid forties, when accommodation begins to go that they find themselves wearing glasses for the first time.

Usually they are still able to see into the distance but need reading glasses.

In time, the short sighted will lose their reading vision and the long sighted their distance vision, producing a double barrelled problem which will inevitably require a double lens answer.

Another problem with glasses is that they get in the way.

They don't go with running through vegetation. I have lost two expensive pairs, both flicked off by springy twigs and sent flying into the undergrowth. Now, I wear a neck cord to hold onto them.

Then, rain splattered or misted up by condensation in humid forest conditions they become useless, more like a blindfold than a visual aid. I often find I can see better without them and finish a course carrying them in one hand or stuffed in a pocket.

Of course many orienteers use contact lenses, but my eyes do not like them.

Even practised contact lens users run into trouble when their accommodation begins to go.

The answer is mono-vision or so I was told.

Mono-vision involves putting a long vision lens in your dominant eye.

You can find your dominant eye by pointing at something in the distance and then closing each eye in turn.

If your left eye is closed and the pointing finger is still in line with the distant object that means the right eye is the dominant eye... and vice versa.

You put a reading lens in the other eye.

Sadly, as accommodation continues to deteriorate you find you can read clearly and you can see anything a reasonable distance away, but some things in between are a bit out of focus and difficult to judge.

In orienteering that means you can't see the ground you are running on, the bumps and dips the boulders and fallen branches lurking in the undergrowth waiting to trip you up.

However, not knowing all that I decided to try out mono-vision.

One-day contact lenses allowed me to use soft lenses for an hour or so in the lead-up and during an event but, and it is a big "but", I had a tendency to build up sticky deposits on them which blurred my vision.

After a few test runs using various combinations of lenses and glasses I finally settled for wearing a reading lens in my left eye while wearing my narrow frame distance glasses. That gave me almost perfect vision in dry weather.

So I bought a supply of lenses and seemed set for better orienteering.

Then my eyes started to hurt. I went back to the optician.

His diagnosis? My long term dry eye complaint was getting worse.

He put me on an eye drop lubricant.

He said, "Stop wearing contact lenses."

He suggested I use varifocal glasses. Look through the top of the lens and I see distant objects clearly. The bottom of the lens is for reading and the area between is geared to ground distance vision.

I don't think much of them but that's life as an ageing runner.

The result was I went into my "perfect run" season back to wearing glasses and still struggling to come to terms with my double bogie vision problem.

4

There would be no stinting myself.

At the start of January, my thinking was that if I was going to get this perfect run then I should compete as often as possible.

The more I competed the more opportunity there would be to chalk up my first PR.

I couldn't do it sitting at home reading a book or watching TV, or even running in one of the forests in my backyard. One of my self-imposed rules was that I could not just go out and visit a few likely control sites on Birnam Hill and say I'd done it. The course had to be set up by someone else and I had to do the perfect run in the heat or under the pressure of competition.

So to get things off to an early start I also put in a late entry for the Edinburgh Southern Sprint towards the end of January, on the Sunday before the English event.

The snow was still lying deep in Perthshire, but it had cleared around Edinburgh so it looked like the perfect warm up for Sheffield the following weekend. It would give me the chance to get a competition behind me and get a run with a map in my hand.

Sprint orienteering has nothing to do with sprinting. It is a short course format usually run in parks or streets based on a ten to twelve minute international elite winning time.

The control features are close together on easy features, and what passes for sprinting takes place between them – short, sharp runs with only the briefest of pauses to check in at the flag.

There was a time when top orienteers shunned such events and venues. They were regarded as events for learners, too easy both technically and physically. The better orienteers let alone the best would not have been seen dead at one.

All that changed when there were world championship titles to be won.

The International Orienteering Federation, in an attempt to find a format that might warrant a place at the Olympics, developed sprint orienteering to bring the sport closer to potential spectators and television. Closer starting times produce a fast turnover in the finish lane, while the shorter running times give a shorter event. Urban sprints – running through city streets, the more maze-like the better - gives close contact with local shoppers as well as spectators. Every November there is a major event in Venice which attracts people from across Europe.

Once upon a time, classic orienteering was orienteering, with top level competitors running long distances, disappearing into the forest to emerge ninety minutes or so later to sprint down the finish funnel and try to snatch top place on the leader board.

Now that tried and tested format has been relegated to a back seat at World Championship level. It is called long distance orienteering. The competitors still think of it as "the classic" and regard it as the one they would most like to win. All over the world, every weekend, thousands of people compete in classic style events.

. "Of course we have to compromise if we want to be on TV," says Norway's 2010 long distance World Champion and Orienteer of the Year, Olav Lundanes, "but I think it has gone too far."

He told "World of O" website editor Jan Kobach, "Orienteers like a challenge. For me long distance is the ultimate challenge because of the training involved and because it is hard to be on top physically, O-technically and mentally for ninety minutes."

That, I believe, not only gives an insight into what to orienteers see as top orienteering, it also gives some indication of just how hard it is for a world class competitor to achieve a perfect run.

The first IOF bid to get over what they saw as a lack of contact problem was the introduction of a short distance format. It has become known as middle distance. A large number of controls in complex terrain with courses just short of half the classic in distance put a premium on detailed navigation.

Then came sprint orienteering.

Now, in all three - long, middle and sprint - each competitor carries a GPS style transmitter which feeds a satellite. That input is used to display each runner's positions on a digital map, each appearing as a numbered national flag, during the events. The display can be seen on huge screens in the arena, on TV or the internet. This gives in-depth coverage for spectators and viewers at home.

Despite all the change, orienteering is no closer to gaining a place in the Olympic line-up.

This is tough on the elite runners in many countries for they can find that any cut back in state funding hits the sports that won't make the next Olympics, hits them first and heaviest.

Some thirty-four sports are recognised by the International Olympic Committee, but rarely if ever do they get a place at the Olympics. There is a strong case for giving all these sports a turn in the Olympic spotlight.

There is of course a case too for the core sports, athletics and swimming, continuing to enjoy preferential treatment with a place at every summer Olympics. They are the showpiece events, the events which the people who are not into sport enjoy watching live or on TV. The others, however, should get rotated so that they all get their turn in the Olympic sun and share the benefits which can come from such exposure – including funding.

It might well be that an orienteering sprint event, perhaps a relay, would fit the bill.

Every year, one of the Edinburgh clubs helps to get the new season underway with an individual sprint event held in line with the international format.

A prologue is followed by a chasing start final, the prologue winner going off first and the field following at intervals determined by their prologue position and timing.

This year, Kinneill Country Park twenty miles or so west of the city, with a mixture of grass and some pleasant forest running and very few paths was the venue.

I opted for arriving and going out early. A late start would have given me every chance of picking up with other runners. That could make the running easier and there would be every chance of following them on the best route choices and into control sites – all legal aspects of sprint orienteering.

I wanted to run on my own as much as possible and force myself to use the map, control my running and make decisions instead of just going round on a wing and a prayer.

I wanted to start the season as I meant to go on.

Besides, an early start would afford me a longer rest between the prologue and the final.

Into the second leg I could feel the first twinge in the leg muscles, not a twinge of pain but just a hint I was running beyond circulation capacity. These early legs were in open park land, flat and too fast.

Incidentally, they used a section of Antonine's Wall – the Roman relic built to protect the empire from the Pictish freedom fighters from the North. It has World Heritage Site status.

I slowed, concentrated on keeping the rhythm and by the time I came out of the next control I was back running easily, picking up the pace a fraction.

By concentrating on the running, I let the map reading slip and chalked up one or two errors over the next few controls.

In particular I forgot to check the route choice options around a small loch where the courses turned at the west end of the map. I found my way blocked by a tough felled area thick with logs and briars and had to take a longer path run round. Then my way into the site was blocked by two or three unmapped fallen trees. I probably lost anything up to a minute.

Now I was into the forest, an area of spruce plantation with little or no ground vegetation layer except in the clearings. The trees were nicely spread out and there was a thick layer of leaf litter..... fantastic running.

The ninth leg to a stream crossing in a deep gully was a great forest run but fallen trees pushed me up the slope and then, ending up too high, I misread the contours around my attack point and lost another fifteen-seconds or so.

Not surprisingly, some of the faster, later starters were catching me up by now, so I went with them, concentrating

32

now on trying to maintain my map reading and my running despite the distraction.

I chalked up another mistake at the twelfth where a small pit was marked as a two millimetre map feature. I failed to adapt to the larger than normal map scale and was looking for something bigger. As a result I ignored one small pit amongst many. That was another minute gone.

Orienteering map scales are huge compared with atlas or road maps. A British Ordnance Survey map has a scale of 1:50,000. That means that every centimetre on the map equals 50,000 centimetres on the ground, or in more practical terms, two centimetres is the same as a kilometre.

Orienteering maps are usually 1:10,000 with every centimetre on the map equal to a hundred metres, or the smaller scale 1:15,000, one centimetre equalling a hundred and fifty metres. The larger scale was brought in originally to help older people with poorer reading vision.

Since then, as smaller areas began to be used in sprint orienteering, 1:7,500 and even 1:5,000 maps came to be used showing more detail and displaying small detail with bigger shapes.

We were using a 1:7,500 map at Kinneill.

The second run that day, the final, was always going to be a hell for leather chase round what was, of course, a different set of controls. The picturesque start was down by the sixteenth century castle, Kinneill House. One of the attractive things about orienteering is that it takes you places you might not normally visit.

I was a late starter this time. You don't run against that calibre of younger opposition and expect to be in real contention.

Again I slowed on the way to the second control, my hamstrings aching for lack of oxygen, but I pulled in the group who had started more or less with me around half way as we headed for marker number seven. From there it was again a matter of balancing running with the opposition, and keeping an eye on the map.

I finished four minutes faster than first time out and ten places up the finish list.

It was a first rate outing with much feel-good running and a not far short of brilliant start to the year.

33

My perfect run was a long way away and would have to wait for another day and another outing.

[See map and course at http://www.routegadget.co.uk – Appendix 1; items (a) and (b)]

5

Life throws up the unexpected, little happenings that seem inconsequential at the time but which prove important as time goes by.

I started running in Kenya at the beginning of my teaching career. Little did I realise what I was getting into and how it would affect my life.

Meru Boys School was a series of block built units with corrugated iron roofing, three double class room blocks, four dormitories, a kitchen and dining room along with five staff bungalows. Cooking in the school and the houses was carried out on wood burning stoves. Electric lighting was fuelled by a generator which was turned off at nine each night. We used oil lanterns after that.

Across one road was the girls' school and across the other was a teachers' training college.

It was about a mile out of town, and a bit isolated.

It was run on the English boarding school model so I was a bit of a fish out of water there, especially with the idea of round the clock duties. Give or take the odd extracurricular activity, I was used to sending the kids off home to their mums and dads come the last school bell of the day.

Everyone in Meru School seemed to take life very seriously, all the time.

I was replacing a US biology teacher who had come to the end of his tour.

One of his extracurricular responsibilities had been to organise the school athletics programme and it was suggested that I might take that on too. Since I was expected to rally round and play a part as well as teaching, this seemed an acceptable option, better than most of the other alternatives.

My own school had always prided itself on its athletics but I was never seriously involved in that. It was an elitist school typical of its day.

There is a never ending drive to get state education back to the supposed good old days of selective grammar and high schools. Many parents fondly believe that their kids will get a better education there – not so at KHS. Everything was geared to the few academic high fliers. The rest of us were also-rans. We got a crack at the whip but nothing more than that.

On the sports field it was no different; only school team players were recognised.

Taking part was obligatory and Harry, the PE teacher, gave everyone a solid grounding in rugby, athletics and other physical jerks, but it was making it into a team that counted and which gained recognition.

I joined the gymnastics club and played the occasional game of rugby for the school but never really made the ranks of the attention attracting squad.

This High School background gave me a sound understanding of athletics and some simple ideas on training which, lets face it, would not have stood up to any rigorous examination. In Meru I started my seat of the pants sporting career as a seat of the pants coach.

The school, on the north-east side of Mount Kenya, had admirable games field provision including a 440 yard grass track.

I remember taking a first walk there using a path through the forest, walking with some apprehension as I kept an eye open for snakes that existed more in my imagination than in reality.

Colobus monkeys and hornbills there certainly were from time to time, as was the occasional elephant.

It was part of Meru forest, much of which was felled and developed as coffee plantations, and for subsistence agriculture as "shambas", as the family gardens were called.

Ten miles to the North it dropped away to the northern plains which were a reservoir of African animal life: elephant, antelope, zebra, giraffe, baboon and cheetah, which we saw regularly on any afternoon safari, plus the occasional rhino, and lion which, sadly, we did not. The pupils at the school had seen little or nothing of this part of their national heritage.

The pay-as-you-go secondary schools in Kenya operated an examination entry system, but it was not uncommon to have elderly teenagers sitting the national KPE primary school examinations for the second or third time before getting their entry qualifications to secondary school. Besides, not everyone had the necessary funding in their family both to go through primary and secondary schools without taking time out. So the average pupil was older than I would have expected to teach on home ground. So too the average athletics ability was higher than I would have found in a group of school kids at home.

There was some real athletics talent, which I must admit, in my ignorance I did little to foster.

Peter Mugambi trained only twice a week during the athletics term but he could run a 4m 20s mile despite the five thousand foot altitude.

Abdul Hamisi could jump over twenty feet.

Joseph Mugambi – no relation to Peter – with nothing more than a strong arm, threw the javelin over 120 feet.

Their season included a Mount Kenya area inter-schools competition and the school sports, but the high point of the athletics year was the District Athletics Championships held at the town's ash athletics track.

Apart from the school team, there were squads from all the main villages in the surrounding area, some of them travelling up to fifty miles to take part, all vying for not just victory medals and the acclaim of the sizeable crowd but a place in the Meru team at the National Championships in Nairobi.

In some ways, this was athletics in the raw. Tiny girls, questionably into their teens, would run over 5000 and 10000 metres.

Don't get the idea that this was a one-horse town event. The district athletics championships were well organised, used quality equipment and enjoyed a turnout and quality of competition which would have bettered many a regional championship in Britain.

The star of the show was a 440 yard sprinter called Mugaa who came from some twenty miles up country to tank the opposition, running just over 49s at altitude for the distance.

Hamisi was the only one of our school squad to win into the team that was sent to the National Championships in Nairobi.

At this time, the first wave of East African athletics greats were claiming international limelight at the Commonwealth Games and Olympics, runners like Kipchoge Keino and Naftali Temu and Amos Biwott. Hamisi was mixing with big time talents.

Established "old world" experts and journalists swarmed like bees around these new stars spawning exaggerated theories to explain the apparent phenomenon and the breakthrough.

To me the explanation was simple. Kenya, recently freed from its colonial past, had a long established system that could find potential athletes secreted away in remote spots, and bring the best of them from across the country to compete against each other in the country's capital.

The new Kenya, keen to establish its identity at international level, went on to develop the best of these quality athletes who benefited from combining training with jobs in the police force or army.

That was a long way from Meru School where my workmates, mostly other ex-patriot staff, picked up early in the athletics season on the idea of "running a mile".

Two of the others were into football but they were no more fit than either I was or that other sports dropout, US Peace Corps man Marlyn.

However, age was on our side. All except Mike, something of a squash expert when he could find someone worth playing, were well under thirty.

A mile was a long way. At altitude it seemed even further. A mile, at altitude, non-stop seemed well nigh impossible. Nobody nurtured any ambitions of doing it fast. Just to run it, finish the four laps of the school's 440 yard grass track was enough.

The soccer men had an admitted advantage. Their legs were used to occasional exercise.

I started off easily – I had to - with jogs down the finish straight.

My legs ached the next day.   Slowly as my tortured calf muscles recovered I moved onto half laps before working up to a complete circuit.

My smoking habit didn't help.

By this time, maybe two or three weeks into our track project, Tony and Mike had already joined the "hall of fame" having duly completed their magic mile. Marlyn went on to do it too, and after a couple of weeks more I did as well, finishing with my heart pounding and that unforgettable flavour of "blood" on my laboured breath, breath which grated like rusty files up and down my windpipe.

The dream accomplished, the others gave up after that, but not me.

I had found something new and little realising how unfit and lacking in strength and stamina I really was, or maybe believing, with all the confidence of youth that these essentials, like fame and running fortune, lay just around the corner, I soldiered on.

Gradually I whittled that eight minute mile time down to around seven and then close to six.

So started a habit that is with me still.   So too started an interest that would ultimately take me into sports journalism and now into writing this book.

It is strange how little and largely unexpected things can influence our lives.

6

Success.

It is more than I'd hoped for and certainly not what I'd expected.

The North of England Championships, the Sheffield area and the Peak District all have reputations that signalled a top class turnout. Host club, South Yorkshire, can claim "best of British" status. Quality facilities and training areas out on the moors attract a quality membership and produce quality runners.

On the day, a quick look at the start list revealed that leading British internationalists and world championship squad runners, Oli Johnson, Graham Gristwood, Pippa Archer, Rachael Elder plus Yorkshire based Australian Grace Crane headed the elite turnout. The age group packs are liberally peppered with past internationalists and British champions.

A stopover in York and then a family drive down with our daughter Nicola and four year old grandson Andrew saw us arrive in plenty of time for our pre-booked late starts.

There is no sign of snow even as we climb out of Sheffield onto the moors to the West.

The sun is shining from an almost unblemished sky but a cold wind hits as we emerge from the car.

Start lists and intervals have been the big orienteering controversy of the international season.

Orienteering, like alpine skiing, some cycling, and in some cases again, triathlon, is a time trial rather than a race.

A race intentionally sets competitors out together and depends on the interplay of the runners, or cyclists, or swimmers to decide the winner. The time, at least in the final, is of interest but it does nothing to decide the outcome and the honours. So we can get fast races with one or more front runners going all out to tame and beat the opposition, and then again we can get slower tactical races with everyone relying on their final sprinting speed to snatch victory, or you can have a mixture of both.

In the time trial, on the other hand, the time is all important, and time trial cycling, triathlon and orienteering all have rules which ban keeping pace with an opponent or following in their slipstream.

Orienteering is different from the others in two ways.

First, because a passed runner not only benefits from a better opponent's running skill by sitting in their wake, they can also benefit from their superior thinking and navigation skills. Most international calibre runners who aren't having to think for themselves will be able to keep up with even the fastest opposition who is navigating as they run.

Secondly, because of the nature of the sport, with everyone picking their own routes between controls, referees cannot be posted, as they are in triathlon, to check if the "no following" rule is being broken.

The 2010 World Championships brought the problem to the fore again as start intervals were reduced to make the event more TV friendly.

People were noticeably keeping up with better opponents who had come from behind to catch them up. Some of them qualified for finals with fast times that again saw them starting amongst the top runners and some of them went on to become medallists.

At most club or even national events, following or, even more commonly, running as a pack, will take place despite the rules. In some cases it is almost unavoidable although it is as well to remember that some if not all the other runners in your "pack" will not be on your course. Chances are they are running one only overlapping your own, and to follow blindly can lead to disaster. You can suddenly find yourself at a control which is not on your list and not on your map. Despite the people around you, you are on your own, so to speak, with no idea where you are – lost.

The entry list posted on the Yorkshire club website had shown that the high turnout over the six classes sharing my course had resulted in the start intervals being reduced from the expected three minutes to just one. It was a same age class runner starting behind me.

I did not like it. The thought of being involved in a hare and dog chase did not appeal. Negative thinking, I know, but I knew from experience that it would be difficult to concentrate on technique rather than "running scared" with someone breathing down my neck.

A few emails later, the sympathetic organisers had given me a change of time and, on the day, the start area is fairly quiet by the time I get there.

The venue is at an upland area called Calver and Froggat, centred on the cliffs and boulder strewn slopes, or "edges" carved out in post glacial times, plus the high rolling moorland to the East.

The opening stretch runs along the foot of the crags dodging in and out and up and over the seemingly endless rocks – thousands of years of cliff fall debris. Not a place for reading the map on the run. The map detail is particularly small and difficult to read in any case. Come to that, this is not much of a place for running – at places I am down to a fast clamber or rock climb. Is there such a thing as a perfect clamber?

Then comes a near vertical run, and I use that word loosely, up through the crags and out onto the moor.

So far, things are going well with only a few minor pauses and a few minor mistakes.

I am orienteering rather than running blind. That's what I'm after.

I hit the rim of the moor at exactly the attack point I am after.

Control six, a low lying knoll scarcely peeping above the long, moorland grass - got it - seven more to go.

Then come the heather and the fairly featureless landscape of Big Moor. I opt for the path option detours – longer going but faster as I get into my stride.

This is bordering on the flawless, running along with both the pace and route under control.

Then coming down off the scarp slope from number ten, things begin to slip away.

As I pass a marshy copse – on the map but with the white almost hidden by the blue marsh hatching, I mistake it for a wood further down hill that I will use as my attack point. Because of this, when I veer off the path I veer off too early. I should, of course, have been pacing the distance and have some idea how far I had run but I had let my technique go. I should have been looking at the map more carefully.

A stop – and how the seconds if not the minutes can slip away as you relocate, find where you are and decide too late the best way to get to where you want to go.

Then it's off down the hill again, running through thick dead bracken and brambles. The path I'd been on would have been so much faster. I should have gone back to it. So that is three mistakes in one control – wrong map reading, poor technique and bad route choice. That would cost me a couple of minutes.

I get number eleven and then twelve and then I'm heading for the finish. This is a shorter course than I am used to and it's strange to be finishing so soon. It gives me a go for broke feeling and that is always dangerous. My mistakes are not over.

Running blind for the "easy" last control, I miss the easy path option, run past the junction and carry on too low forcing a late climb within sight of the finish. Another minute gone.

At "download" my printout showed a time of just over fifty-two minutes and a class placing of first, two minutes up on the Hereford man in second. There were still a few to finish but with my late start it seemed likely that I could hang onto my position.

So it proved. The on-line results giving the split times for each control showed I led the field from the start.

It was success, a real confidence booster, but I had made orienteering mistakes, failed to adapt my running style to the changing conditions.

Not a perfect run, no, but it was a win.

[See map and course at http://www.routegadget.co.uk – Appendix 1; item (c)]

7

I have never been a natural at running.

Increasingly even the best runners are being taught to run better but in my time scale, that is all new.

Runners like me who have never had a coach have to pick up pointers where we can.

Often these pointers have come from watching my betters in action either live or on TV.

I watch a lot of sport on TV – almost everything but football, cricket and formula 1.

I also watch a lot of athletics.

In the first two months of the year, I picked up a couple of bits of running perfection on the "box", as Edinburgh hosted its annual international cross-country in January and then Birmingham staged the Aviva Indoor Grand Prix.

In Birmingham there was a high quality turnout including Cuba's Olympic hurdles champion Dayron Robles, but for me, the final track event with Ethiopia's Tirunesh Dibaba, Olympic Champion at 5000 and 10000m, attempting to take the world record in the rarely run two miles was the most perfect run of the day.

She took over the lead as her pace setter dropped out after six or so laps but she was already running to perfection with Kenya's World 5000m Champion Vivian Cheruiyot, giving chase.

The Kenyan lost it three laps from home, her rhythm just losing its edge. She recovered to come again over the final three hundred metres and chase Dibaba home.

The Ethiopian always had the race and her opponent under control, with her early pace, her cruising mid-race, her final acceleration and her last lap sprint all run with perfect technique.

Edinburgh had a layer of snow on Holyrood Park for the X event.

I can remember a time when cross-country running meant just that, with courses likely to take in grassy fields, rough pasture, stubbled winter fields, ditches, hills and even the occasional farm track. It could be tough going in the wet and even tougher going when the frost had turned the rough ground into a "pebble bed".

I can remember too that the top runners of the time took all that in their stride.

It was all too much for the "blazer brigade" officials at IAAF headquarters and when they took over the sport, country running lost much of its magic. They wanted the best of top track runners to become cross-country runners, and despite the strong European tradition for just that they feared that many would not risk their high earning potential and ankles on the traditionally rough terrain.

Park running became the norm and in 2009 the World Championships reached an all time low with most of the course on dirt roads. It was, in truth, road running.

A whole new younger generation is growing up in the sport believing that this is what cross-country is all about. I'm no dinosaur. If people want park running, let there be park running, but why not have cross-country running as well?

What is needed now is a new sport of Real Cross Country taking in the most runnable fields, forest, rough pasture and moorland. As traffic builds up on roads making road racing increasingly difficult to organise on a small scale, maybe the Real X season could be extended through the summer as well.

Edinburgh's Holyrood Park offers the best that the IAAF format can offer, with a steep if small hill called Haggis Knowe covered in rough grass providing an often decisive tester.

January's snows had threatened the event but the course was runnable. That said, the difficult going proved too testing for pre-race favourite, World and Olympic Champion Kenenisa Bekele.

Kenyans Joseph Ebuya and Titus Mbishei left the Ethiopian struggling, with apparent ease.

They cruised along to finish first and second, Ebuya, a former World Championship silver medallist at 3000m, accelerating over the final descent to make sure of victory.

Both had looked superb. What I noticed in particular was that they ran with bent knees throughout. There was no reaching for the ground in front as you see some runners do as they try to increase their stride length. It was almost as if the angled joints were supplying extra springs absorbing the pace from each stride to spill it out again behind them to maintain their speed.

I'm not suggesting they were running differently from other top international distance runners but, on the day, I noticed it and I kept it in mind.

Cross country running, even in its sanitised IAAF form, is about as close as track athletes come to orienteering. For a start it is more chaotic than track or road running, and it involves running over a considerable distance.

Just the time factor alone, running for thirty to forty minutes, makes the chances of a perfect run less likely.

Of course when it comes to looking for perfect runs over distance you must start with the Ethiopians.

Bekele and his predecessor as world number one on the track, Haile Gebreselasie, gave the world a whole new insight into what distance running is about with their exploits in the decades before and after the turn of the century.

They inherited an Ethiopian running reputation which started back in 1960 with Abebe Bikila's barefoot marathon win at the Rome Olympics in a world record breaking time.

The picture that thrilled the world was of the shoeless African, a soldier in the emperor's bodyguard, ignoring the rigours of both the mind boggling distance and the cobbles and tarmac of the Italian city streets to trounce the opposition and win. It appealed, in a romantic way, to the popular image of the African runner, a simple, untrained man with no more than natural talent, bettering his city spoiled opponents. He was the first African to win Olympic gold.

Probably the best of all time - Master Runner Haile
Gebreselassie. A sub-four minute miler who broke records
at 5000m 10,000, and in the marathon
(SCC Events/Victor Sailer)

Another Ethiopian running great, Gete Wami in action in Berlin. (SCC Events/Victor Sailer)

He went on to win the title again with another record breaking run in Tokyo four years later.

On the track, Miruts Yifter, was the first Ethiopian to attract world wide acclaim.

"Yifter the Shifter" as he was known, following his race winning tactics of putting in the occasional searingly fast lap to burn off the opposition, was unbeatable from the middle seventies and into the eighties.

He was favourite to win both the 5000m and 10000m at the 1976 Olympics in Montreal, but Ethiopia along with many other African countries staged a boycott because the International Olympic Committee had refused to exclude South Africa which was still controlled by its white supremacist "apartheid" regime.

He made up for that four years later in Moscow when he won both titles.

By that time he had refined his technique, content to sit in until the last lap and then using his sprint to telling effect.

In the 10000m he beat Finland's Montreal winner Lasse Viren, finishing twenty metres clear of the field after surging to the front with three hundred metre to go. His final four hundred metre lap was timed at 54.8s.

Viren only ran really well at Olympics. He was a specialist in "bend mathematics", keeping the distance to a minimum by keeping close to the inside of the inside lane on the bends. It was claimed that he improved his fitness by using blood transfusions to increase his red blood cell count. It was not an illegal technique at the time and it was never more than speculation.

Yifter won 221 out of 252 races during his career.

Into the 1990s Gebreselassie, burst on the scene with double distance victory in the World Junior Athletics Championships in Seoul. Like Yifter he had remarkable last lap speed.

In the 10000m in Seoul, the long time Kenyan race leader pummelled him on the back in frustration as he went by with just metres to go. The next year he won the senior 10000m title and later that year he broke the six year old 5000m world record.

A small man at 1.65m (5ft5ins), Gebreselassie cast a long shadow that put every other distance runner both then and before, including Yifter, in the shade.

1995 has been described as his Milestone Year. He not only retained the 10000m world title but broke no fewer than six world record indoors and out.

He went on to win four consecutive world titles and two Olympic titles at 10000m.

That was his distance; he broke the world record four times and finished his track career with a best of 26m 22.75s. He was a runner of top international standard at event distances from 1500m to the marathon in which he knocked the world record down to an awe inspiring 2h 3m 59s ..... inside thirty minutes for each of the ten kilometre splits. He has said, he made mistakes that day. It was not a perfect run.

As he himself predicted, he lost his world 10000m crown to fellow countryman, Kenenisa Bekele.

The younger man had claimed two Olympic 10000 m titles by the end of the "noughty" decade, and he also won at 5000m in Beijing. At the World Championships he won the 10000m four times, like his predecessor, and he has taken the 5000m once.

Moreover he has bettered Gebreselassie's records over both distances and his success at cross-country shows him to be the better man when confronted by tougher going.

From '02 to '06 he won both the long and short World Cross-country Championships. After the short event was discarded, he won the men's title in Edinburgh in '08.

He has been injury prone, having Achilles trouble in 2002, hamstring problems in 2008 and a calf injury in 2009 and 2010.

The Ethiopian women emerged onto the international stage later than the men.

Gete Wami set them on track with her World Championship win at 10000m in Seville in 1999 and two World Cross-country wins.

It was Tirunesh Dibaba who set standards between 2003 and 2008 despite losing out at the Athens Olympics. She completed the 5000m/10000m double at the Beijing Olympics and at the World Championships in Helsinki. In the 5000m, at which she finished the decade still holding the world record she took in 2008, she won the world title both in Stuttgart and Paris and she took the 10000m too in Osaka in 2007. In addition she won four World Cross-country titles. Like Gebreselassie and then Bekele, she ranks as the most prolific winner of her generation.

Gebreselassie, Wami, Bekele, Dibaba and all their fellow country people who are knocking at the door of the world number one slot are all perfectionists in style.

Long distance specialists, they can all produce world times at distances from 1500m upwards and in all likelihood those who have yet not done so will be able to follow Gebreselassie and Wami in becoming marathon runners of note.

In addition they can all show audacious sprinting speed, an ability derived from the perfection of their running style.

They all may have their off days, witness Bekele in the snows in Edinburgh in 2010 and the humid heat of the World Cross-country Championships in Mombassa two months later.

It could well have been that the calf injury which kept him from the track season that year was at least partly to blame.

However, they all embody running perfection.

The thing about distance running is that it gives you every chance to appreciate it to the full.

Orienteering boasts its own menu of running giants.

None come bigger than Switzerland's Simone Niggli who has dominated the women's sport since winning her first world title in 2001.

By the end of 2010 she had won seventeen individual world titles despite taking a year out to have a baby. She took all three individual titles, sprint, middle and long, in 2003 and 2004 and was in the winning Swiss relay team in both these years.

She has won forty-seven world cup series events, medalled twelve other times and won the overall series six times in the decade.

Her success has gained her full professional status in Switzerland where she is in demand to appear at a host of commercial public relations events. She is widely recognised in the streets of her home city and she has been Swiss Sportswoman of the Year three times.

Is she the best ever? On the face of it, it would seem so but her career has been affected both by the number of titles which can now be won at a championship and the move to have World Championships every year.

In addition, her professional status, earning at least as much as she would have had she taken up her prospective career as a biologist, has given her a long competitive life, taking part at world level into her thirties.

Back in the days when there was only one individual world title available at each championships and at a time when the championships were held every two years, Sweden's Annichen Kringstad won in '81,'83,'and '85, dominating the sport over six years before retiring at the age of twenty-five. The pressure of feeling she had to win spoiled the sport for her.

She was the first Swedish orienteer to gain national recognition winning the gold medal awarded annually by national newspaper Svenska Dagbladet to the country's top sports performer, an honour she shares with tennis ace Bjorn Borg and athlete Carolina Kluft amongst a number of other internationally renowned Swedish sports stars. She was also Swedish Sportswoman of the Year.

She came back to work in orienteering in 2010, taking up a media relations role aimed at raising the profile of the sport.

It remains an open question whether the diminutive Kringstad would have bettered Niggli either head to head or on record if the sport then and now had been organised similarly and she had remained competing into her thirties.

On the men's side, which some argue throws up closer competition by weight of numbers if nothing more, Norwegian Oyvin Thon won two titles in a row, was silver medallist once and then finished seventh three years in a row before his retirement in 1987, without doubt a formidable record in competing at the top of the world.

Peter Thoresen of Norway won two classic gold titles, in '89 and then again eight years later in '97, and he won another, this time in the new short distance event in '93. He is now a leading international level coach.

Sweden's Jorgen Martensson, who now regularly wins his class at the Masters World Championships, won two world classic titles, in '91 and '96, and silver in '97.

Martensson, competing before the development of middle distance orienteering, found himself struggling to make his breakthrough in classic distance. He concluded that he needed long distance running stamina and he changed his training accordingly.

His first move was to cut out what is now known as cross training. He gave up cycling and cross-country skiing, commonly used by Scandinavians during the snowy winter months.

"The only way to train for running is to run," he says. "If the snow was knee deep we still went running."

Of course, there are many competitors across sport who find that cross training works for them. British swimming sprinter Allison Sheppard peaked late in her career after she had substituted land based weights sessions for a substantial quantity of her high weekly swimming mileage.

Martensson also toughened up his running sessions.

"We found the toughest bits of forest and did our interval training there," he says of the small training squad he worked with in those years.

It worked.

French ace Thierry Gueorgiou faces now a similar problem, for despite his success in middle distance and sprint running, out of five long distance outings, his best was silver in 2009 while he won bronze in 2010.

Perhaps he could learn from Martensson's example.

All of them, however, are formidable sports people who run and navigate to perfection.

Whether they maintained perfection over a full ninety or so minutes of world level pressure is another matter.

Switzerland's Daniel Hubmann, another of orienteering's world greats and possibly the fastest forest runner of his generation, says he has chalked up a number of perfect runs in his career.

Hubmann took up orienteering at eleven but shared his running time with athletics until a World Junior title convinced him he should concentrate on orienteering. Nevertheless, he has slipped inside 66 minutes for the half marathon.

In the last three years of the decade he has, arguably, dominated orienteering. He won the World Cup in each of them. In the same period he won eight individual World Championship medals including long championship gold in '08 and '09.

The Norwegian terrain in 2010 seemed to place him at a disadvantage, for while he shared bronze with Gueorgiou in the middle distance, he finished seventh in the long. However, he would not be the first non-Scandinavian to find that and he won't be the last.

"I haven't done it that often," he says, "of course it's a goal but it is a high goal to reach."

He adds, "In sprint racing, where you can count every second you can lose, it is easier. I did it in the World Cup final in Zurich."

In 2009 he won that sprint by a massive sixteen-second margin with his time of 14m22s, after being fastest through eleven of the twenty-four controls and rarely more than two-seconds down on the best into any one of them.

The previous year he had scored another Perfect Run winning a middle distance world cup event at the Swedish Multi Day O-Ringen. That success came despite his competing for the tenth day in succession and a very unusual setup. The runners travelled to a high hill start in the ski lift and then ran down on a circuitous course which included a number of difficult cross slope downhill legs. He beat Gueorgiou into second by just three-seconds this time with his time of 31m38s.

He told press officer reporter Eva Jurenikova, "I was tired but I pushed hard from the beginning and had a perfect race. It looks an easy area but you had to read the map carefully all the way."

There's a lesson there for all of us and for me, more than most, with my perfect run ambitions.

Four of the Best

1 Daniel Hubmann (Switzerland) - World Middle Distance
Champs qualifiers in Norway 2010
(Photopress/Alexandra Wey))

2 Thierry Gueorgiou (France) Into the finish at the
2010 World Cup
(IOF/Niels-Peter Foppen)

3.Simone Niggli-Luder (Switzerland) - Another gold - World
Long Distance final in Norway 2010
(Photopress/Alexandra Wey)

4 Minna Kauppi (Finland) The middle distance title "in the bag", the 2009 world number one anchors her team to relay gold. (IOF/Pirjo Valjanen)

8

February is the month for colds. I should not say, "The month" because November is a month for colds too. Usually, I have two colds a year.

Martensson says that during his heyday, he put January aside for having a cold. To his way of thinking, he believed that in the average year he was going to go down with a cold at some time, and rather than waste valuable training or competition time he had his annual cold during his January break.

It sounds like a chicken and egg situation. Which came first, the cold or the belief he would have a cold? He maintains it was the belief and I can understand that.

Most of the time, I have an almost indefatigable protection against colds based on will power and paracetamol.

When I feel my nose begin to itch, inside not out, the first sign of an approaching cold, I take a paracetamol and then begin to think it away. I repeat the process if necessary. The next day the symptoms are usually gone.

The scientist in me puts it down to the placebo effect but so what, if it works. Placebos are a pretty strong medicine.

Taking paracetamol on its own does not work, nor does deep thinking.

It rarely works for colds which start in the throat or chest.

That is what happened in the second week in February; my throat felt raw and there was a cough developing. I knew an unavoidable cold was on the way. Just how bad it was going to be was not yet clear.

Following on from the North of England Championships I had gone back into training.

There was still some ice on the forest tracks but my training is varied, and even in better conditions, I can, and often do, keep trail running to a minimum. Much of my time I do cross-country forest running, building up strength and stamina in the muscles used in the rougher forests.

I have often heard road runners complain of disappointing performances when they take to cross-country running for the winter season. They equally often admit to doing little or no soft terrain running on grass or fields in preparation for the switch. The saying goes that there are horses for courses and just as a horse trained on dry turf is always going to find wet going difficult, so a road trained runner who sticks to the tarmac is ill prepared for the country.

A road trained orienteer is ill prepared for coping with the forest floor.

Equally well, you will get road runners who are surprised, even embarrassed, at how badly they orienteer. People who would not road race without the training miles behind them think that because they are runners, they can pick up a map and orienteer without training either their muscles to take on the new style in terrain, or their thinking so that they can come to read a map at a glance and translate it into the country around them.

That is not the way life works.

Gordon Pirie, the Olympic silver medallist at 5000m, was one of a group of British world class track runners who became a serious orienteer. His fellow Olympians from the 1950s, John Disley and Chris Brasher, who later went on to set up and organise the London Marathon, coaxed him into orienteering which had just got underway in England largely at their instigation.

They were both steeplechasers. Disley, from Wales, won bronze at the '52 Olympics in Helsinki and Brasher, who helped pace Roger Bannister to the first sub four minute mile, won gold in Melbourne in 1956.

In a 1957 Observer article, Brasher wrote, "I have just taken part, for the first time, in one of the best sports in the world. It is hard to know what to call it. The Norwegians call it "orientation".

A Swedish initiative had got orienteering on the go in Britain in 1961 with a first event held near Edinburgh. The first Scottish Championships were held the next year in Dunkeld on Craig a' Barns (which as I can see from my back garden) and the Scottish Orienteering Association was set up the next day.

Orienteering in England was still in its infancy when Disley organised a series of events in the London area in 1964.

Brasher, who became the first chairperson of the newly formed British Orienteering Federation in 1966, competed at these.

Pirie, who broke the world records at both the 5000m and 3000m in the summer of 1956 before going on to take Olympic silver, was one of a number of top runners pulled in, in an attempt gain media interest in the new sport.

In his first event he found his running skills counted for little and, it has been said, completely lost, he had to ask a passer-by to show him the way back to the start.

He went off to learn the skills of map reading and navigation and became proficient enough to win the British Championships in 1967 and again 1968.

Internationally, he is probably the best of the world's track runners to have come into orienteering over the years, but when he went to the World Championships in 1966 he finished forty-sixth.

Two years later he had moved up to twenty-eighth position, but over an eight mile course he was still over forty minutes down on Swedish winner Karl Johansson.

At neither event was he best of the British, but he was best of the British track athletes taking part.

That is a mark of the difference between these two sports for runners. Yvette Baker, who won gold, silver and bronze at world level for Britain in the 1990s, underlined what makes orienteering runners different when she said, "I can read a map on the run as well as I can read a book."

So I don't just practice running, I practice forest running and navigation as well. I like to get off the trails and into the woods. I can take an "O" map with me and practice reading on the run, reading the terrain around me and picking off rocks, crags, summits and other likely control features.

Midway through a session I will have a rhythm going, loping, if that is not too strong a word, through the woods if the going is good, picking up and using a deer track for a spell when the legs begin to tire or the vegetation gets really thick underfoot. I'm sure to have the odd pause to check map detail, struggle through some rough ground, or to recover from a fast spell or maybe an uphill grind, but by the end I don't feel the cold of a winter's day, I'm sweating, and I know I have been running.

That doesn't mean I don't run the trails to get up my long, slow distance mileage.

Birnam Running Club was in operation throughout February and as with the rest of the dark winter nights we used head torches to find our way in what can be the blackest darkness under the trees. It can be hard going on some of the stonier paths and with my history of Achilles problems I usually have to slow down.

Like many orienteers I don't tally up my training distance in miles or kilometres. I measure it in time. All roads and tarmac paths are much the same so although running rates may vary the distance is pretty well a spot on measure of effort. That isn't so in forest running where the underfoot going can sap your energy over a one hundred metre stretch and have you flying along over the next. Time is a much better way of totting up your training effort.

I had done about eleven to twelve hours in January, despite the conditions and I wanted to build on that. Elite runners in their prime will do that and more in a week. Their bodies can take it. If they can't they fade out of contention and the limelight.

As February got under way I would be out most days for maybe forty minutes to an hour with the occasional longer session of up to ninety minutes. From time to time I would do a weights and machine session in the gym. In the first two weeks I had just two days off.

On the first Saturday of the month, Fife Athletic Club, who put on a prodigious event calendar every year, staged their popular Tortoise and Hare team race. Since it is a trail race four of us went along from our running club.

The format saw the two person relay teams – one slow runner and one faster – cover a two mile forest trail two times over.

This non-stop country running is hard going when you are used to the go fast go slow interval approach of orienteering.

I started my first lap slowly, probably too slowly, and got some reasonable stretches of rhythm going but my legs were under demand long before the home straight.

I thought the between lap break might cause problems, but no, I was quickly into my running again, keeping it well within my aerobic limits while working to keep up my stride rate and knee lift, and ran it faster than first time around.

The whole event, on top of a week of hard training, was a very tough outing.

On the second week of the month there was another fun outing, to Pitlochry this time, for orienteering.

One of the Glasgow clubs, STAG, used Faskally woods to stage its Knoll Kollection event. There was a control marker on every hill or knoll in the forest and the idea was to check in at as many as possible and get back to the finish in one hour.

The Scottish Night Championships had been held on the Saturday but with my eyesight I had given up on night eventing way back – I don't do night orienteering.

Come Sunday morning, a cold Sunday morning, a field of sixty-five set off from a mass start - unusual in orienteering. Surprisingly, it didn't take many minutes with everyone going their separate ways before I found myself running on my own and continued in that way over a large part of the circuit. Again I got into my run fairly early, and while I made a few early navigation mistakes and finished nine minutes earlier than necessary, I enjoyed what I saw as another training outing rather than a competitive outing.

Two days later I copied the night event controls from the internet and went and did the circuit again. I was fairly happy with the time too.

It was the day after that the dreaded cold virus struck.

Running was out of the question. Apart from anything else there is well documented evidence that if a virus such as this infects the heart muscle then you are dicing with sudden collapse and possible death.

Besides, it was time for a day or two in bed, if not to speed up recovery then at least to make living less uncomfortable. The snow had returned. With a hidden layer of ice beneath the new fall in many places, going out was not pleasant.

Then Katharine succumbed as well. We were a miserable pair.

After a couple of days I seemed to be on the mend and was all set for a return to training when the virus returned with a vengeance. Some days it would disappear altogether while other days it felt like flu, aching limbs one day, high temperature another and a pulsating headache on another yet again. I had been given a flu vaccination but swine flu was at its height at this time and I have wondered whether that was my problem. Folklore says, "You know when you have got flu," but surely different people respond differently to the flu virus just like any other.

It was a frustrating time. I missed out on four events, three of which were perfect run opportunities with club events at Darnaway on the Moray coast – Darnaway is a beautiful forest full of shapes, really excellent running and the venue for the 1978 World Championships - a park event in Edinburgh and the Scottish League opener staged on the dune terrain at Gullane on the south side of the Forth estuary near Dunbar. The fourth was very much on home territory on Newtyle, another Dunkeld hill I can see from my back window. It is tough going in places with steep stretches and deep heather and while I might, if all went well, navigate a course there without mistake, I very much doubt if I could ever go there and run to perfection. I rarely if ever train there and I had few regrets about missing this South League event.

On one of our better days the sun was shining so we set off for a scenic tour of the Highlands driving up over Drumochter Pass to turn left down the Laggan Valley to Fort William. It was all very beautiful especially since another four inches of snow had fallen in the north-west. All the mountain crags were etched to perfection showing up a dramatic black and white while the great round shoulders of the hills in other parts caught the light and stood out against the blue of the sky. The snow lay deep on the branches of roadside trees.

After coffee at Spean Bridge, we dropped in at the Aonach Mor ski centre and took the gondola lift to the upper slopes. This was a first for us. It is strange how you can miss out on things like this despite many visits to the area until one day you ask, "Why not?" and make the decision.

It was well worth the trip with a remarkable panorama of peaks circling the horizon starting with close by Ben Nevis, Britain's highest summit, just a few miles to the West.

It was Monday and possibly some weekenders had stayed on, but in any case the slopes were busy with skiers, snow boarders and people on sledges. It all looked so easy, as they came gliding down the various pistes. A few walkers using one or other of the high level routes passed by. A Swedish tourist group with their own radio team was putting together a piece on Scottish skiing. They had spent the previous day in Glencoe and seemed impressed.

We headed for Glencoe after lunch and completed the circuit by way of Crianlarich and Loch Earn.

In all, eighteen days went by before I felt fit enough to go out running again.

March 9 says my training diary – forty minute jog by the river. Great day but it's a long way back.

I was back. Things could only get better.

That Saturday I went out on a small club event at the Hermitage. It's one of my favourite training areas so I know it well. Even technically difficult controls and the tricky north end of the map were not as testing as they should be. In places like this mistakes come from too much self belief, thinking you know the area too well to bother with the map.

Bravado more than common sense saw me opt for the longer of the two technical courses which included a heavy uphill section towards the finish.

After that with a kilometre and two control sites to the finish my legs felt dead and my head, if not exactly spinning, was a not very sure where my feet were. I was not as well as I thought I was. My recovery still had some way to go.

9

Men of a certain age meet other men of the same certain age undergoing the same routine of tests that come with a suspect prostate – PSA blood tests, digital examination with a finger up the rectum, prostate biopsy with a "gun" up the rectum, occasionally, a camera up the willy.

I didn't need that, or at least, I didn't want it.

What I really needed was competition, not just because that would give me more chance to chalk up that perfect run but also because I had to gear up for bigger events ahead.

Into March and there were some major events on the horizon.

My eye problem, however, had produced other unexpected consequences.

I followed up my last visit to the optician with a visit to my doctor for a second opinion.

That was OK by him, but he said, "While you are here, I should really check out your blood pressure, and take blood and urine samples to check out cholesterol, your prostate, kidneys and liver function. A general check up."

In truth I had been trying to avoid this but I went ahead. Saying "no" might make it seem like I had something to hide.

The blood pressure seemed on the high side but I almost convinced him that it was a bit of "white coat" syndrome, a test induced affect.

I went off with a "home" monitor and returned a few days later with better, more acceptable readings.

After a week or so the results came back from the blood tests.

Liver and kidney function were OK. Cholesterol and the PSA level were both on the high side.

The cholesterol and blood pressure readings were put through a computer programme that seemed to ignore my salad lunches and daily running work load. It decided that I needed statins - a group of chemicals that help to prevent the blood vessels clotting up - without a daily statin intake I was doomed to die – twenty-five per cent chance of going before reaching eighty.

There are not many optimists in white coats.

I think, a twenty-five per cent chance of dying really means you have a seventy-five per cent chance of survival.

An internet search of my own found another Scottish cardiovascular risk evaluator that also considered my diet and exercise lifestyle and increased my chance of survival to eighty-one percent.

Let's face it, we are all going to die, but I went on the statins in any case.

The PSA result was something else again.

PSA – prostate-specific antigen - is a chemical released in the prostate gland during semen production. Some of it passes into the blood. Cancer in the gland, the major killer in men, boosts the level but so too does swelling of the prostate, benign hyperplasia as it is called. Most older men are likely to suffer from this to some extent. Middle of the night pee excursions are an almost sure sign.

Sadly, above normal readings can be indecisive, which is why there is no population screening for prostate cancer in men.

However, get a higher than "normal" reading and the threat of cancer is there.

Nothing can take over your life like the cancer threat, returning at unexpected moments to nag at you like the proverbial disappointed spouse for not giving it your full attention.

You go into the cycle of test and test again with little or no chance, it seems, of being given an all clear no risk message ever again.

Some get prostate cancer and die….I have run with men who have done just that - under treatment in the winter, gone by the tail end of the summer.

Others get it and never know it.

There are aggressive forms which are quick killers and not so aggressive forms which never show themselves.

Most just go on from year to year and test to test.

I had given myself a four year break - a string of family occasions had not seemed worth disrupting with a potential health scare – but here I was back on the circuit again with the same nagging threat.

The consultant's report was again encouraging.

I kept running. The quest was still on.

In the middle of the month, I headed north to Aboyne for a small event in the town's Bell Wood.

It was the first day of Spring. There was a chilly wind but the strong sunshine bathed the car park and it was good to get out of the car and feel relaxed and warm. Did a hard winter mean we were going to have a warm, dry summer?

Since it was a small area, well known to many of the local runners, the organisers gave the option of using a map with a difference – none of the paths or tracks was marked on this version. Not only did this mean you had to rely on contour and vegetation shapes for navigation, but when you hit a path it tended to pull you off line.

I went for it. It meant much off-path running and produced a major mistake halfway round when I overshot the control area by maybe three hundred metres. The major forest road which I crossed and which would have been a first class stopper was, of course, not on the map.

It is another lesson for life. Try something differently and it is like trying something new or for that matter, look at something from a different angle or view point and it can look completely different.

Every time I drive up and down the A9 it looks different. Different light, different weather, different season, even different time of day and it comes over as fresh and new.

A circular walk is always the more attractive option, but it is surprising how an out and back walk, instead of producing boredom can have views seen only minutes before come up with surprises.

It is a reminder that others can have a different point of view and can look at things differently, not just when they are looking at the world around them but at the things that are happening in it too.

That doesn't mean I am going to agree with them but it should mean that, barring killing, cruelty, inhumanity and basic unfairness, I appreciate that my view and opinion are not the only ones.

The next Saturday I went to Stirling's Touch estate to the west of the city for one of the UK Cup events – an elite senior and junior geared series which supplies courses too for the run of the mill competitor.

It was a middle distance event, which made little difference to people like me for even the veteran course was no shorter than my usual circuit.

Where middle distance is different is that the courses use complex terrain where they can criss-cross their way from start to finish with a high density of controls sites.

The forested slopes at Touch are ideal for this with a series of knolled ridges fanning out from the high terrain to the South West.

Visiting the same area doesn't make it much, if any, easier especially if you are coming in from a different direction and view point.

At the start I am feeling relaxed and ready. By now I am getting used to the idea that I am here for a perfect run and not competitive success.

Control number one – I take it carefully, getting my eye in to the terrain.

Two – the long seven hundred metre leg. The ground is rugged rather than rough. It means you have to adjust your running to suit, adjusting the stride length, going down a gear as it were, when necessary, rather than using the accelerator, but you can keep the rhythm going.

A curving sweep to the right avoids the climb and leaves me with a minor "in the circle" adjustment to hit dead on.

Three – A short run, avoiding the hill top and some rough going - the green hatched area on the map – and I am still on target.

Four – four hundred metres or so and all is going well until I hit a path on the ground which isn't on the map. It is covered in grass and so technically might not be a track, but it is flat and you could drive a car along it. The one on the map is further on, over the next spur but I turn to follow this one until stopped by a high fence. I relocate and go on to negotiate the really difficult terrain around the marker.

That's my perfect run hopes blown again. Now the objective is to make this a "one mistake outing".

I reach number ten with a minor miss into number seven the only other blemish, but then go haywire.

Like most of these "shorter" events the course takes us on a run through the finish field.

From ten I should be heading west again back into the woods but I mistake the control I can see further down the hill as my next and go running down to what turns out to be number eighteen, the penultimate control on the course.

Just as well no one is watching me. That's one of the benefits of being an ageing wrinkly rather than a young top dog.

They make mistakes too, you know, but then people tend to point fingers.

I sneak unnoticed through the nearby gate and running against the tide of early finishers set off on a long uphill path run.

Any hopes of a through the woods short cut are prevented by the high fence. It means a detour of three to four times the real distance. I push too hard in a bid to make use of path running and go into oxygen debt.

At last I reach the far end of the enclosure and turn into the wood. I was in this area not many minutes ago going for "four" but that doesn't help; it is tough orienteering and I don't recognise much about it.

That's not always true. Sometimes an area is etched on your memory by past disasters.

It's like that on the easy stretch from twelve to thirteen where I had gone badly adrift the year before.

This time I take care to pick the right valley as I climb out of the burn at half way, follow the marsh and then cross the ridge and go into the re-entrant beyond.

Orienteering obviously isn't all about highs and elation. Hitting that re-entrant to find it empty, without a kite, carries a punch-below-the-belt level of disappointment that is surely unmatched in sport. Most sporting reversals can be seen coming or at the very least bubbling up as a threat.

That too can be true in orienteering, but many are wicked not just because they are unexpected, but because they are a completely against expectations. You think it is going to be there. You are sure it is there, and, it isn't.

Number thirteen carried an extra thick larding of disappointment, for when I returned to the same point for at least the second time and after five minutes of relocating on this and that feature, I found the marker right there, where it had always been, sitting behind a fallen tree. I had been too quick to assume I was not where I thought I was.

From then on it was hard to get geared up again to pushing it on the way home but, all expectations gone, I put in some of the best legs of my day.

In the distant past when I was forty plus and feeling my age, it never failed to amuse me how some older people, usually women, would call me "son".

"Would you hand one of those down for me, son," someone might ask in the supermarket.

I can understand that now.

At Stirling, much of the opposition in the veteran field were boys in their forties or early fifties. Even without my mistakes I would not have been very high up the results list.

They had a big advantage over me and the other more mature guys in the field. I am not just manufacturing excuses. There are well documented reasons for this. The passing years affect the body parts, not least the cardiovascular system – heart and blood vessels - in charge of supplying energy to the working muscles.

Again it is the lack of elasticity to blame.

Heart muscle "cells" contain an elastic molecule called titin.

The name titin comes from the name of the supposedly gigantic, mythical Greek gods, the Titans.

In other words it is a massive protein molecule, the largest in the body. Its chemical name, and amalgamation of all the chemical bits and pieces, is said to be the largest word in English with 391,319 letters.

Titin's elasticity doesn't just play an important role in contraction of the heart, it makes the heart supple and allows it to stretch, important when it is being filled with blood between the contractions that send the blood out to the body.

Titin content is reduced by ageing. The heart loses elasticity, takes longer to fill and to empty, which is probably one reason why the maximum heart rate decreases with age.

Elasticity of the artery walls also plays an important role in circulation. The artery walls stretch allowing the vessels to take in the blood pushed out by the heart and then, as the heart relaxes, they contract to push the blood on and into the waiting tissues. The elastic protein involved becomes compromised with age, becomes less stretchy and less able to contract. This means that blood flow to the tissues is slowed and the heart has to exert a higher pressure.

It also seems that resulting damage to the elastic tissue can have further damaging effects, stimulating thickening of the muscle layer and artery blocking deposits.

As far as the ageing runner is concerned, it means a reduced oxygen supply to the muscles, running slower, earlier breathing problems and anaerobic misery.

This is why age groups have become the norm in orienteering, triathlon, and road and track running.

The downside of this is that they take away any excuse for a bad result.

So it was at the age group event the next day.

Touch was part of a weekend double. On the Sunday we were off further west past the tourist hot spot of Callander to the Trossachs.

The Trossachs, the hilly wooded area surrounding the end of Loch Katrine is another tourist hot spot and deservedly so, for it can lay strong claim to being Scotland at its most beautiful.

I cannot forget the time many years ago when orienteering on the slopes of Achray Forest to the immediate south. As I burst through a belt of thick trees into a ridge top clearing I was stopped in my tracks by the breath stopping view in the valley below. Ben Venue to the left, Ben An across the valley, both rising above the rugged oak forest covered slopes that nestle beneath the summits between Loch Katrine and Loch Achray immediately below.

I have seen the view many times from other vantage points but this is the one that sticks in my mind. Orienteering as they say, takes you places other folks don't reach.

As far as orienteering is concerned, the Trossachs is a place to get lost in, a place where making the map fit the ground needs much imagination and much simplification, a place that stops the first time visitor in their tracks. I can well remember my first time there, jogging out from the start map in hand, standing gob-smacked thinking, "Where now?"

Now I know it slightly better, but the rugged, rough terrain with much heather, rough grass and marsh; the climbs, the descents, the crags, and the route choice are still nothing short of daunting.

Conservation concerns had forced the planner to make late changes including the siting of the start area, so I set out on a course not dissimilar to the one I ran last time out around a year or so before. That didn't make it easy but I knew a few mistakes to avoid.

So I start well.

At control three my compass bearing coming off a steep little ridge takes me towards what I think is the wrong little hill but I feel I must check it out before turning down the valley to find the marker.

Was it a mistake? It was more of a reasoned, reasonable decision. Let's put it this way, if the rest of the run is perfect, it is the sort of check out decision that I would be tempted to ignore. In my mind I'm still going for a perfect run.

The next control is tricky but easy by Trossachs standards. I enjoy the up-slope run, pause to take my bearing as I dip into the next valley and then head up the other side into a smaller valley on the right. Spiked it.

Then comes a longer leg and the temptation is there to head straight, going along the twisting and buckled slope heading in that direction.

I control the impulse and opt to follow a nearby marsh which goes most of the way. The trouble is there is a hill in the way. I cut back the way I have come and avoid the hill and the climb, turn right through a small break in the ridge and hit the marsh as expected.

With a brief check of the map I set off.

Running marshes can be hard going. A number of the top runners consciously adapt their running to cope with them.

Swiss ace Simone Niggli says, "If you push too hard they use up your energy." She reduces her drive.

73

Daniel Hubmann, a ball of the foot runner in most circumstances, runs the marshes on flatter feet possibly to give better grip, certainly to reduce sinking and spread the push.

As I run along Beccy comes in from the right. She had been at the last control just before me and had opted to climb over the hill to reach the marsh. That was one up to me but then she works her way slightly higher up the side of the valley and pulls away from me. Maybe she has found a deer track. I have kept by the stream which trickles through the bog to keep on track and find I have to negotiate a few minor water falls.

Walkers are warned against following hill streams in the mist because waterfalls can prove a dangerous problem.

Beccy is getting further ahead. By the time I turn the bend with maybe just one hundred and fifty to go she has disappeared.

Forget it, I remind myself and run on to hit this one too spot on.

A broad valley lies between five and six and a stream of people can be seen running across it and up the other side. From the marsh in the bottom a deer track heads in the right direction. I take it and climb first one steeper slope and then the second to hit the really steep spur where I am looking for a small re-entrant beneath a sizeable crag.

There's the crag and here is the dip with the kite nestling in it.

That was easy.

The next offers a classical up and over or round the bottom of the slope option.

I go for the latter and follow another marsh up the valley and then take the steep little climb to find the hillock. Beccy passes on her way down after going over the top.

I miss the direct line on the next short one hundred metre leg and have to turn into it to find the hill and then lose further seconds locating the marker.

No real mistake there, a minor bump on the side of the hill can throw you a fraction off line especially if the detail is difficult to see, but it unsettles me.

I opt for the direct south west run to the next, failing to notice the valley lying slightly behind me and running west on a wide detour that might offer easier running.

I have to negotiate some steep descents through fairly dark woodland – the sort of place that can still make the hair on the back of my neck prickle. It does, but I ignore it and try to keep up the pace and plough and slither on down to meet the marsh at the bottom.

I negotiate round a steep little hill, hit the big marsh I am aiming for and crossing it at its narrowest hit a deer track. Deer aren't stupid. They usually pick the easier routes.

I follow it round the side of the hill, find the next valley and go into my control from the small marsh. That's another fine leg.

Ten is a short leg. I'm looking for a knoll where the slope opens out. From there, the objective is to keep height on a slope which winds in and out of the hillside on a short run to the next knoll. There's no problem; no problem bar finding myself on top of the knoll with a crag-like drop to the marker. I am running on a high by now and I launch myself off the edge, take a couple of strides, hit the level and spike it.

I detour to the right on the next short leg close to the road crossing. On the way to the start we had passed this crossing and I had noticed then the steep slope rising behind the spot where the control was obviously hidden away. Pre-warned I was ready for it. My detour took an easier descent and I notched one of the faster times of the day for this leg.

I have been navigating well and despite the rough terrain and thick undergrowth, I have been running in cruise mode.

This may not be on target for a perfect run but it is certainly close to it. A run to be pleased with. A run to be proud of.

It is easy going from here on to the finish. Relax. Concentrate on the running. Go for a fast time.

Next I know I have taken the wrong turning where the route leaves the road and goes back into the terrain.

I am looking for a track from a minor car park. There's the car park. There are a couple of cars around and there are people.

It throws me. I turn sharp right following the small tarmac road rather than the track going straight ahead. I run the best part of sixty metres before I realise my mistake. Too embarrassed to run back past the people in the car park I turn left to plough across a grotty marsh to reach the path further along.

Then, thrown completely, as I round the small hill to the left, I ignore the marker I see in front of me and head off up the next little hill to look for it over the top of that one. I only run twenty metres before I realise my mistake and turn back but that's over two minutes lost on two mistakes at one easy control. It is so disappointing. All right, I have already lost maybe five minutes, but that was on really rough going over some of the most difficult orienteering terrain in the world, let alone the UK. To throw all that away in a few minutes of mindless carelessness is unforgivable.

No doubt about it now, I've blown it again. No perfect run here.

Two more controls and a perilous, fast, down path finish gives me a time of just over sixty-five minutes, fifteenth place out of seventy-two starters, first in my class and quite a few notable scalps.

[Touch - see map and course at http://www.routegadget.co.uk – Appendix 1; item (d)

Trossachs - see map and course at http://www.routegadget.co.uk – Appendix 1; item (e)]

10

Every sport has its big occasions. That's true over the whole range of competition, everything from the local club Grand Prix series to World Cup events and World Championships.

The JK is Britain's premier event of the year, held every Easter.

It is a four day, international, memorial get together named after the young Swede who did much to encourage the sport in Britain in the 1960s, Jan Kjellstrom.

His father was founder of the Silva Compass Company.

Sadly it is rarely referred to as the Jan Kjellstrom festival even on the official programme and most often called quite simply the JK. Surely a commemoration event should do the honour of remembering the person's name?

In 2008 a Friday sprint event was introduced to the programme, and it always finishes on Easter Monday with the club relays.

The men's relay winners collect the Jan Kjellstrom Trophy, but the Saturday and Sunday elite and age group time trials are the centrepiece of the event, the total times deciding the overall winners of each, with the elite, of course, taking centre stage.

Importantly, while a few contestants may opt out either because there are family holiday arrangements that take precedence or simply, on occasion, it is too far to travel, most of the top age group runners from each region are likely to be there.

Two days of competition doubles up the pressure with every possibility that a second day disaster will wipe out a good first day run, and conversely there is every chance that a

77

brilliant second day will see you leap frog the opposition to score a major success – relatively speaking, of course.

Success and failure in orienteering are all down to how well you run compared with the people just about as good or bad as you are. It is like road running or cross-country or cycling for that matter. Only a few competitors are in with a chance of winning. It is all about beating or losing out to the guy you knocked your pan in racing last time out and maybe the time before that. Strong racing friendships are often welded between rivals finishing well down the results week in, week out. Other times they are rivalries which are only rekindled once or twice a year at major events like the Jan Kjellstrom.

The JK venue moves around the country, each regional association taking its turn at organising, so this year it was hosted in Devon with top class running ground at both of the main venues.

I was looking forward to it.

Let's face it, following that early success at Sheffield things had taken a downturn.

For starters, there was the snow and ice which continued to ruin the running at home. It did not clear from the trails until well into March.

Then there had been my repeated colds and my eye problems.

I was out to reverse the downward trend. A pleasing result of any kind was the boost I needed.

So……..

Individual event Day 1 - it is wet. It has been raining all night. Parking is in another nearby plantation forest and Katharine and I walk in the rain to the assembly and finish area. We both have early starts shortly after 10 o'clock.

The field is under an inch of water which is rapidly turning to mud as the gathering crowd walk through it.

Just after we arrive the rain eases and finally goes off. That's a turn up. With any luck, I think, it will stay off for my run.

The start is the best part of a kilometre away, so with maybe forty minutes to go I plant my bag under the tarpaulin we have brought and set off, allowing time for a warm up and to take in the start area. A sea of mud marks the turn-in from the farm track into the forest. No point in trying to avoid it, everything is going to be wet and dirty by the end of the day so plough on through.

I continue my warm up close to the start and then with ten minutes to go I clear my digital control recorder and spend a few minutes taking in what the current starters are doing.

The start kite is maybe twenty metres away at a ride junction and can be easily seen, which isn't always the case. Everyone is going down to the kite and turning right. Then gradually one or two cut into the forest earlier. However, they soon disappear into the trees.

Then it is my turn.

The pre-start covers three minutes. I check in. Check my electronic "dibber" and wait for the timer to beep.

When it does the runners up front get underway. I move forward into the second "box" and pick up my control descriptions list and fiddle it with some difficulty into the holder that slips over my wrist.

This is an aggravation I could do without but as yet they haven't come up with anything better or I haven't come up with a way to use it efficiently.

The clock beeps again. I move into the next box where sample maps are lying to give a preview of the competition area.

Lining it up with the compass puts you into context with the start even if you don't know where the start actually is on the map.

If it is the first time you have ever seen the map, it also gives the chance to pick out any path network if one exists, the main contour shapes and any other features that might prove useful during the run.

The area is a gentle slope running east to west. There are a number of gullies, a few tracks. The vegetation is varied, a mixture of open felled areas, and plantations, some of them thick some not so thick.

Route choice and following it will make the difference.

The clock beeps again and I move to the start line.

An official points out the kite and how the maps are laid out in their boxes. I'm on course twenty.

The clock beeps again and this time I'm off.

I pick up my map, check it is the right one. Occasionally a wrong map gets into a box and occasionally some poor sod has to come back to the start when he finds his control ID numbers don't match up with those on the ground. Some have even completed the wrong course only to be disqualified.

So I have got the right map. Next I check the general shape of the course. Is it a simple circle or straight line or is it a tricky one, twisting and turning and maybe crossing over itself? It can also be useful to be aware if the course includes any special areas.

I am already on the move as I take in the first control. I already know from the control description list that it is a vegetation change. The map shows it is next to a large thick bush – a circle of dark green "fight".

There is no easy route to it but it is just around a couple of hundred metres away through the strip of forest to the right and across a rough open area.

The bloke ahead is moving away from me, moving faster. I am on the point of picking up the pace but think again. Forget him. Concentrate.

I hit the open felled area and find a deer track that makes for easier going.

Hitting the edge of the forest I look to the left and can see the control.

A woman is coming back into it. She must have missed it first time around.

Check the control number. OK. Check in with my dibber.

I already know that the next control is back along the edge of the open area but a look at the map shows a ditch in an area of thicker plantation. It is about five hundred metres away as the crow flies. Following the edge of the felled area would take me right there, with the chance of a short cut across where it widens out just after half way.

The mud is really thick there at the edge as the ground is already getting churned up by running feet. I keep my running technique, plunging straight into it and lifting the knees, but it is heavy going and I know this is going to scupper me for fitness later in the course.

The rough ground further out is really rough and not an alternative.

I opt instead for the forest to my left, crossing a steep hedge bank and turning right on the other side, moving over to avoid the thick mud developing there.

Then it's on with the running. Concentrate on style. Check the map from time to time.

Cross the fence. Tick it off mentally on my map, and then the same distance again through a thicker bit of plantation until I meet another bank. Check. Cross and turn right to skirt the next block of conifer plantation keeping it again to the left.

It's muddy but manageable. Not too many people have come this way.

The wood here is deciduous, an old coppice that has been allowed to go wild.

Pleasant area but the trees are twisted and angled making for chaotic running.

I reach the mildest of bends in the plantation edge. This is my attack point.

I have already noticed that the many dry ditches all emerge into the wood where I am running. Mine is the third one once I've turned the corner.

I carry on, counting as I go. One. Twenty metres. Two.

Just a minute there is a control down there. Could be mine? Its unlikely two would be on similar features so close together. Worth checking.

I race down the ditch and check the number. It is mine.

Later I find that my first ditch was just on the other side of the bend so my counting was out of synch.

That is enough of an upset to break the routine.

The next control is a ditch junction in an area of open plantation but there is an area of thick "fight" between me and my destination. I'll have to go round it.

I opt for the South side, back out into the open wood briefly, then head through a small open area and into the other wood, turn north to hit the long ditch, then follow it to the junction. That's the plan.

Later I find that I have made the decision too quickly without checking the alternatives.

There is a road to the North. Looks like a hair on the map so maybe that's why I missed it.

It is a slightly longer route but it is could make for faster going and as it turns out, affords a safer attack point.

I angle through the plantation. It is easy going. I hit the open woodland and turn left to follow the new block of plantation. The clearing comes up. It is scrubbier than I expected. I pause for a moment then force myself across it heading north east to search out the long ditch in the new block of forest.

I reach the edge and find a north running ditch.

That's it. Follow it.

It is that first lesson on life that comes from orienteering – you will always jump to conclusions.

I set off until I hit a thick area of young spruce.

Now we come to the second one. The second lesson on life is it is hard to admit you are wrong. It hard to say, "I have made a mistake". What a wonderful world it would be if we could all – politicians especially - say just that.

A nagging voice keeps telling me, "This is wrong."

Another says, "Don't slow down. Carry on. Must keep moving."

Into the fight I go, struggling deeper and deeper until I come to a stop. I take control again at last.

This is not a ditch I'm following, it is a stream. I should not be in "fight".

I jump the stream, put my head down and force my way through to the open forest beyond.

Where am I?

There is a road down the slope to my left.

I check my map but my detour has left me not quite sure where I am. I'm still running scared.

I turn south and run up the slope looking wildly around until I hit a dry ditch. It must be the one. It is running east to west as it should be, but I'm not quite sure.

I turn east and run on. There is a marker ahead. I go for it. Check the number. It's mine. Relief.

Back home a results check shows I lost at least a minute with my mistake and probably at least one more by my route choice and missing out on the road option.

So that's just three controls down and eleven more to go and…….. another bid for a perfect run has already bitten the dust. Now I'm going for a result, but a result won from using the perfect run format.

Four is just a hundred metres away across the bend in the road.

The map which had been jumping up to meet me before seems awfully far away and everything on it looks awfully small. I can't make out what feature the circle centres and I forget to check my control descriptions.

It is close so run on. Just make sure I am running in the right direction.

I haven't settled, that's the problem, haven't recovered. I should have stopped, checked the map briefly but carefully and then run on at speed. That's the way a mistake can throw you.

Across the road I'm slow, hesitant. Number three and my mistakes are still taking their toll.

There's a woman ahead going behind a couple of upended tree roots.

That's it. Pick it up, Go for it.

That was quick after all, not so bad. I'm feeling better.

So now I have turned at the east end of the course and have that heading for home feeling.

I start picking off the features on the map and keep an eye on the compass.

Almost at five and there's Pete ten metres or so ahead. I have caught him up several minutes but the Manchester runner is nursing a very bad knee and limping.

We go our separate ways with me on a rough bearing ploughing through some thick underfoot brashings, and despite his injury Pete makes the control before I do.

We both follow the ditch out of the forest block heading for a large clearing a couple of hundred metres away.

Time to take in the map.

I head off on my own to negotiate the big gullies part way, one with really steep sides.

I pause just for a minute then decide – bite the bullet – step it down the crumbling slope and clamber up the other side.

There's much boys-in-the-wood action in orienteering. I think it is one reason I like it. I've never really grown up.

Turning left I hit the clearing - it looks more like a small field.

Where's the marker?

That's it on the far side.

So six down, eight to go.

So it goes on shrugging off the temptation to follow the herd before picking up a really small clearing at seven, running a difficult contour and compass leg to eight, navigating into a tricky number nine and all the time adjusting my route and running to take account of the changing vegetation and underfoot going - sometimes firm, other times marshy, occasionally grotty.

Then comes another tree root but this time it is one of a dozen or so in the area.

A couple of streams pull me off line and after crossing a felled patch, I enter the wood higher up the slope than I would like.

A fair sized "fight" area is my attack point. I hit it and aim off.

The physical effort of running through the stretches of mud is beginning to take its toll.

I see a couple of roots. Can one be mine?

A couple of runners are heading that way. I run in and spike and with a brief look at the map head off up the slope on rough compass.

I pass a marker at a ride junction, pick up the point on the map and run on.

Some runners are heading further west. For a moment I am tempted to follow. I waver, but then I hold to my line.

There's a ditch. Mine is the second one. I hit the marker dead on.

Now I am just navigating by the lines and shapes on the map. That's the way I like it.

By now, close to the finish, runners are funnelling into the area but their controls could be very different from mine.

I wander off course to twelve but probably use the better running to reach the field.

A quick look to the left at the field edge and I weigh up the angles, and then run across to hit the next spot on too.

Out of the wood, up the field and back in again. I can see the marker from thirty metres out. That's thirteen.

Then I'm heading for the gate to the finish field and the final control.

It's up hill, not a big hill but at the end of a heavy run it makes for very heavy going.

I spike and then try to sprint up the water logged finish lane.

I'm running well but running slowly. The air is like treacle around my legs.

I clock out at 50m4s, a sub 50 run so close but so far.

At the end of the day I take third just eight-seconds down on the winner – first Roger, second pre-race favourite Arthur and then me.

The three of us were just a second apart at thirteen after Roger lost three minutes finding what was surely one of the easiest controls on the course. That's what can happen when you are tired and under pressure. We have all done it.

I'd lost out coming up the hill and again on the run in.

[See map and course at http://www.routegadget.co.uk – Appendix 1; item (f)]

11

So there I was, all set up for a Day 2 tilt at the title. Wouldn't that be something? Win my class with a second day perfect run

I won a short course JK title many years ago.   Most age group competition offers long and short courses for each class catering for those who, probably because they are not putting in the fitness training required to step up in distance or maybe because they have family commitments, prefer a forty minute run rather than be out for an hour or more.

That success was spoiled by a poor loser. The man who had expected to win grumbled that one of control markers was in the wrong place. You just don't do that sort of thing. You might think it but you don't say it.

A few years ago I took fifth over two fine running long distance courses in Yorkshire. I was flying, both days, but I was beaten by faster men.

So, I turned up at Braughton Burrows the next day ready to go for gold, as some of my sports pundit friends might put it. All I had to do was forget about winning and go for a perfect run.

But, and it is a big capital lettered BUT - that plan did not take into account a readiness I have to see doom lurking around every corner.

Braughton is one of Britain's most extensive areas of sand dunes with four high ridges separated by valleys. Most of the system is backed by a large flat area scattered with smaller dunes and dune slacks, marshy in places but deep in water in others.

I must admit to a few qualms about running in dune areas, the more so if the vegetation is not thick enough to protect them.

Some in the conservation lobby complain about orienteers running in wild country.

A number of investigations by highly qualified ecologists have shown that at even in the biggest events any damage is short term.

Swedish orienteering has a policy of designating wild life buffer zones in a competition area in a bid to save elk in particular from the pressures that a big human running presence can induce. A team walks through the forest before the event to move the animals into the safe area.

Newly colonised dune areas are particularly susceptible to damage with the microscopic fungal life which binds the sand together, preventing blowouts, being destroyed. So I question if they should be used.

Braughton has long been a military training area. The Allies used it as a preparation zone for their assault on the beaches of Northwest France in the 1944 Normandy Landings and it is still widely used by all from foot soldiers to tanks.

It already has at least two massive blowout areas so a day of orienteering is not going to make much difference.

All the regular military use means that it is criss-crossed by numerous tracks.

It is also a popular walking area so there are many smaller paths.

The pre-race info says that not all the tracks are marked on the map and that many of the marshes will be under water.

It is a bright dry day, but a snell westerly off the sea hits you as you get out of your car.

Arthur, yesterday's runner up, has an early start and finishes shortly after I get there.

He has a not far short of excellent sub-49 minute time for the five kilometre course.

He is a Cornwall man so he will have run here before.

That's going to be hard to beat.

Should I be thinking about winning? I should be concentrating on that perfect run and treating any other success as a bonus.

It is all of 1.4km to the start.

I am scheduled for just after one o'clock with Roger due to take off just three minutes before me.

I am warming up on the pot holed, earthen road that acts as the waiting area when he arrives and moves off to get himself ready away from the others.

Some people like company at times like these. Others prefer to be on their own.

His start time comes and is about to go when he arrives apologetically but late and is hurriedly moved up to the correct pre-start box.

Is that his first mistake of the day? Not the sort of mistake I like to make but, I must admit, a mistake that paled into insignificance alongside what waited for me out on the course.

Then he is off.

Will I see him again? I thought.

I start well despite the flooded marshes and the widespread areas of burnet rose which keep forcing me off course.

I slow as I come to grips with the map, skirt the first dune and run into number one.

As I run round the edge of a huge marsh deep in water, one man full of youthful strength and bravado plunges on through with the water well above his knees.

I follow a road before striking across country to hit two. (I'm fastest of the day at this one as it turns out).

Two marshes and some nifty map reading later I spike number three. (Third fastest in my class).

I reach number four still lying second overall and as it proved, over a minute up on the time posted by early leader, Arthur.

I don't know this and a combination of marshes and the prolific rose stems have forced me off line again on the way there.

I relocated quickly but I had left more than a morsel of self confidence lying bleeding and injured on the way.

I didn't think I was doing well although with all my experience and hours looking through results I should have realised that other people would be making mistakes in this terrain.

However my shoulders were beginning to drop. In my mind I was already a loser.

Cool it, I say, but I don't quite manage. Every impulse is to get the head down and chase it.

I cross the nearby style, pick up the road on the other side and look into the jungle of small dunes and a veritable maze of paths ahead.

The map shows them all but so much info becomes none. It is more than the brain can cope with. The crucial slope contours are lost amongst the clutter of circular dune shapes.

As for the paths, while they all look the same on the map it quickly becomes clear that they are far from the same on the ground. Some are grassy. Some are not. Some are twin tyre tracks. Others are single. The maze of dunes and depressions in amongst them make the going even tougher.

I know that often in orienteering, path navigation is my downfall. Usually I come off at a bend at the wrong angle or at a bend that is not even on the map.

However, on the day I forget this. I should run round the area to pick up an attack point – the bushy dune to the East, say. Instead I decide to plough on across trying to follow the tracks.

I can feel I'm on a high, but not the right sort of high. The adrenalin is gushing and caution is slopping like water from cupped hands as I run.

I pick a path up the left hand side of the area, one that cuts across to a major junction. Get there and I can go on the compass over the final hundred metres to the control site – a depression well shielded by sandy hillocks and all deep in marram grass. What a scary control.

I reach "the junction" and move as planned into the dunes but....... it's not there. The control's not there.

If it's not there and I'm not where it is, where am I?

So started thirty minutes of thrashing around. Neither paths nor land shapes made sense any more.

Suddenly everything on the map becomes very small.

I go back and come in by the paths to the East.

Once I back track over three hundred metres to a distant watering point and come in again only to find myself just as lost as before.

This is the sort of thing that has people give up orienteering.

Twice I say enough is enough, drop out, don't complete the course, head for the finish.

Twice I argue myself out of it. Most tellingly, it is an awfully long way to jog home.

I try a different tack. There are areas of bright yellow on the map – short grass on the ground.

Here's one. It must be that one, or is it? Maybe it's that one over there.

There seem to be short grass areas all over the place.

What exactly did the mapper mean by short grass?

I look at my watch. I have been out over forty minutes.

All chance of even relative success is gone.

It's an admission of failure but it is an admission that takes all the mounting tension away.

I can almost feel it slip from my shoulders.

Then I notice a big area of "sand" on the map. It must be high on the ridge. Looking up I can't see it but it must be on the other side of that high point I can see.

That gives me a relocation point. I head up the slope towards it never intending to go all the way there but to pick up a path about two hundred metres up, a path that heads straight towards the control point.

It's there. The path. I hit it turn left along it until I reach a really major junction.

I'm there. I pinpoint it on the map.

The control, I tell myself, should be just in here.

I compass in and lo and behold, there it is. Check the number. It is! It is it! I've found it!

Later analysis of the leg showed that on that first assault half an hour or so ago, I had failed to pace-count my way along the paths and had made my first turn too soon.

Furthermore, I should have been climbing both to my intended attack point and again from there into the control and I was not.

Moreover, I had gone from what I thought was the attack point into an area of dunes that was far too small, much less than the one hundred metre form side to side as shown on the map. Probably I was in the triangle of dunes immediately to the South, but with major mistakes like that you can never be sure. All the information was there on the map. All I had to do was take the time to read the map and use it.

I would like to say that that was my final mistake of the day but it was not.

All the coaching manuals tell you that right then – just after an error - is the time to consolidate.

If I had looked out across the plain below me and used my compass I would probably have been able to pick out the dune which carried my next marker just two hundred metres away.

I use my compass OK but then I just run on down the slope without taking that crucial look at the land ahead.

Too soon, my befuddled brain is struggling to cope with too much vegetation, too much dense vegetation, compared to the map. It is bewildering.

The contours are also confusing. Contour lines are either solid or dashed. The solid ones are at 5m intervals. The ground between them rises by five metres. Any ground shape between contour levels or extra height above a pile of them is marked by a dashed line, or "form line" as it is called.

My problem here, although I didn't know it until later, is that the mapper has used high tide level on the beach over a kilometre away as his base line and not the flats I am running over. That means that quite small dunes – including the one I am looking for – just happen to break the next five metre line and are marked with solid lines. They give the impression of the wrong height, and often the wrong shape. Dashed lines giving their true shape would have been, shall we say, more helpful.

So on I run towards a far, high dune forgetting again about pacing the distance.

After two hundred extra metres I reach the hill, run up it and of course nothing is there.

Dejection. Misery. I control the spate of expletives welling up. They would only hasten the slide into chaotic thinking.

I head back to the path almost to where I started the leg.

It really is time for some careful thinking.

I'm at a path junction. Right, found it. The map shows a row of three big bushes. I look up. There they are. Follow them.

I set off, slowly. There's a woman coming from the left. Ignore her. One bush, two, three. Now turn right. "That must be it over there," I say out loud, run over and up the knoll – not even up to head height – and "there it is".

"Just what I was saying," says the woman who has followed me over.

Having got on terms with the bush mapping, or rather the lack of it, I run on to take in controls seven and eight.

Not for the first time I find that the stop-go routine, standing around with my head buried in the map, had left my legs running empty, badly in need of another warm up session.

It is heavy going until I get back into gear on the climb to nine and from then on it is back to normal dune orienteering – look ahead, pick out the major features, head for them and fine orienteer into the control.

Despite minor errors I am again up with the best of them over seven to fourteen - third fastest to number thirteen - but there is no making up for those mid course errors.

I am thirty-fourth out of thirty-nine on the day and nineteenth with my two day total.

Arthur takes the title.

Roger, after running into major problems at number four was twenty-fifth on the day and eleventh overall.

Save for our major errors we would both have finished in the top three but then that is orienteering. Running fast is important, but it is not always the fastest runners who win. It is the people who keep control and use the map, make the right route choices, and find the controls who claim titles. Everybody finishes their day saying what might have been, everybody that is bar those who have had a perfect run.

[See map and course at http://www.routegadget.co.uk – Appendix 1; item (g)]

12

The odd thing about sport is how things come up trumps when least expected.

A couple of weeks after the JK I head fifty or so miles north to the Spey Valley for a small event run by the local club.

All the disappointment of the Devon event is behind me.

The disappointment had nothing to do with losing; I am used enough to that. It was not even the disappointment of not doing my best. Otherwise getting a perfect run would be a run of the mill affair, something I do every time or every other time out. It was not even the disappointment of doing badly. No, it was the disappointment at losing control, letting myself down.

A number of years ago British orienteering imported Swedish coach Goran Andersson to be their international squad director.

British team runners report that a main plank of his approach was to get his runners to think on the bright side after finishing.

What is it the old song says? – accentuate the positive, eliminate the negative and don't mess with Mr. Inbetween.

Well, that wasn't one hundred per cent the Goran approach, but his approach to producing top results if not winners was designed to build confidence. Heather Munro, the first non-Scandinavian to win the Swedish O-Ringen international multi day event, a winner at world cup level and bronze medal winner at the World Championships and World Games, said that she owed much of her success to Andersson and the self belief he gave her while working with the British team.

Andersson built a post race routine which started with looking for the pleasant things that had happened. Only after these aspects of the run had been analysed did he get around to talking about the mistakes made.

It was an approach which produced dividends.

The Scandinavian, it is said, finally tired of the admin side of his job, reportedly largely a matter of jumping through paper hoops to satisfy the money providers at UK Sport and Sport England. He left Britain and went on to meet with some coaching success with both Swedish and Norwegian teams.

His was a hard recipe to follow in the minutes and hours after my finish at Braughton, but once the dust had settled and I had drunk a coffee or two, I did just that.

Number one positive was that I had finished despite temptation to throw in the towel.

Number two – I had used the map.

Number three – apart from some notable exceptions, I had relocated well when necessary.

Number four - I had been reading the map well despite its drawbacks.

Number five – I had controlled my running.

The mistakes were easy to list. I had not used the map as much as I should have to simplify the route through bits of complex terrain. I had not always picked attack points. I had not pace measured my running, so when I needed to I did not know if I had gone too far or not far enough.

Finally – when the chips were down and I felt up against it I had panicked.

When I panicked I did not orienteer.

The day after, while still in Devon, I had got back into training.

At home again the training continued with much map-in-hand running on fairly complex terrain. I don't always use a map of the area I am running on, using whichever map I take with me to develop and practise reading on the run, or on the jog to be more precise, getting into the habit of visualising the control and the route to it.

The Dunkeld area is brilliant for orienteering and training. It has one of the best areas in Britain in Craig a'Barns. That, plus Drumbuie, Craigvinean, Ladywell and Crieff Hill, all mapped and on my doorstep mean I am spoiled for choice, while easy outings to Pitlochry, Blair Atholl and beyond plus a number of woods around Perth break the monotony that might come with too much of a good thing.

So I am feeling fairly relaxed as I head up the A9, over Drumochter Pass, down into the Spey Valley – despite the rain - and head for the Ralia Centre for a coffee and pre-race nibble.

Kincraig is a small village, mainly a new development centred on a tiny hamlet, about ten miles west of Aviemore.

This whole area is rich in mapped orienteering terrain.

The bit around Kincraig seems less than promising – a strip maybe five hundred metres wide at its best, partly built up and with a road and a railway running at right angles to each other through the middle.

All these drawbacks pale into insignificance when you get out there running.

It is nothing short of a delight with open birch woodland on morainic terrain full of dips and rises, terrain covered in the main with a mixture of short heather and grass underfoot.

I stepped up in distance to 6.6km and what a course it proved to be!

Neither the occasional path nor the stretches of village street at the start, in the middle and again towards the finish did anything to detract from its "gem" status.

Into my run I have picked up a rhythm early on and feel I can do this forever.

OK, Ewan McCarthy, a British team contender until his career took him offshore, is going to tank me.

Let's face it, it would be a big disappointment for any experienced competitor in his mid-twenties if he could not. I am running well and if my technical game is up to calibre then a perfect run is on the cards.

On the way to controls two and three, I waver off-line but these are not mistakes and come well within the boundaries of acceptable variation.

The detail on the map is getting bigger all the time.

Tennis players "in the zone" say the balls are like footballs they are so easy to see and play.

In orienteering it is the map that gets magnified by the adrenalin that comes with hitting top form.

On the path run towards thirteen I check out the next couple of controls ahead. The terrain is opening out with some grazing ground and patches of wood. The next is in the open to the left and then it is on over to the wood at the south side of the map.

The climb to thirteen is tough and maybe for the first time I am running outside my comfort zone and breathing heavily to cut the anaerobic deficit.

A runner I've pulled in over the last two controls spikes just ahead of me.

It is a situation that from experience should have set warning bells clanging......tired even if just for the moment and concentration eroded by the other man.

I set off for the "next control" – a second hill in a long stretch of wood.

Partway there and something is wrong. I'm running at the right angle from the map but it is the wrong angle on the ground. There's the wood. Just run for it.

I check the map again. Yes, there it is number fifteen.

Wait, what happened to fourteen? It should come after thirteen.

I look at the map again.

Yes, fourteen is where it was the last time....... in a shallow valley in the open to the left. I am heading to the woods away over to the right.

I panic, but only for a moment.

From where I am the control is almost level. I check the map again. Look back to thirteen. Look at the control again and go for it.

Well, that's my perfect run chances gone again but hey, lets make the most of this, chances to run in an area like this come rarely.

Two controls later I cross the road and run into the woodland at the east end of the map using the path as I begin to feel the past four kilometres of fast running begin to ask questions of my legs.

I look to the left to check my next route into the trees and the next control.

My foot hits a stone and next I know I am lying on my back and hurting.

I don't fall like I used to. These days I am down on the ground before I know it. No stumbles no wild gyrations in a bid to keep upright, just straight down. Fortunately, six times out of ten I still manage to turn over to land on my back.

I sit there.

A foot to the right and I would have tumbled down a really steep slope.

My hands are bleeding but there's no time to sit and feel sorry for myself.

Sucking the blood from the wounds on my finger, I'm up and on my way.

Round the turn at the end and I'm heading for home but the pleasant open forest lures me into a couple of route choice mistakes that will add a few minutes to my time.

Underfoot, it is slightly heavier here and a couple of path runs would be faster.

Doug goes by. I remember him many years ago when he ran as a fifteen year old. Now his son is that age.

He must have been in trouble. He was pulling me in at number four and here we are heading for twenty-one.

I finish in 65m14s, a close second amongst the older veterans. That's sub ten minute per kilometre pace.

Ewan clocked 36m27s.

Just two mistakes and my running was more-or-less perfect. Things were looking up.

13

The British Championships, held traditionally at the beginning of May, are like the JK in that they move around the country.

This year it is the Midlands who play host at Cannock Chase, just fifteen miles or so north of Birmingham city centre.

Out with the Lake District, it is probably the first English area I competed on back in the 80s and I was here again back in 2005 for the JK. Then, I was on a fairly high beta blocker dosage and all I can remember was struggling on the hills on my way to a middle of the field finish.

The Chase, the training ground of a number of top British performers over the years, mainly coming from Peter Palmer's Walton squad, is a mixture of forest, plantation and heath covering two or three square kilometres of plateau.

Teacher Peter Palmer was another runner who came into the sport with Pirie and his ground breaking athletics friends.

The forest is the home to a number of herds of fallow dear and the rare nightjar.

Not that I have seen one. It would be on a really bad run if I saw one of them in nocturnal action.

It is a designated Area of Outstanding Natural Beauty dating back to 1958. Its structure and vegetation owe much to the underlying sandstone which drains the thin soil leaving it largely infertile.

A series of deep but largely dry valleys cut deep into the plateau. This terrain, the relatively easy going in some places plus a network of paths, puts route choice at a premium.

Over the centuries building rock and sand have been quarried. It was once a coal mining area and deep fissures always present a danger and while much of this land is a no-go area for orienteering, the bit to the South that remains on the map is rich in difficult control picking features.

The Midlands have a bad reputation with some folks, based it would seem on its industrial past.

The rolling vistas, stretching towards the Welsh hills in the North and the Malvern's in the South, are rich in woodland and pleasant agricultural landscapes putting the whole area high on the list of Britain's most beautiful countryside.

Birmingham, or the city centre at any rate, with the concert hall, museum, city square and a tangle of updated canals that once served England's industrial heartland, has become one of the country's better and most attractive urban areas.

It is a lively place with its numerous well landscaped bars and restaurants attracting a crowd of well dressed revellers and if they become a little too boisterous at times then it probably means it is well past your bedtime.

The only bad thing about the Midlands is the M6 although it must be said that attempting to travel through the region without it would be well nigh impossible.

Our trip down was unforgettably bad, the problems starting well before we were anywhere near Midland territory.

Opting to detour a major M6 hold up by taking the Manchester ring road at rush hour was a poor "orienteering" decision.

We reached Walsall after 8pm and after booking in at our £19 a night hotel and eating at a local pub we went to bed.

Any ideas I had of a trip into Birmingham City centre to eat and take in one of the canal side pubs along with a spot of jazz were ditched.

One of the canal side pubs has in the past proved a source of some lively music.

Over the years I have established a habit of searching out the music spots while visiting cities at home and abroad either for work or, as in this case, pleasure.

In Seville for the World Athletics Championships I found a bar where real flamenco was available on a nightly basis.

This was not one of the many costly tourist trap venues in the city with flamboyantly dressed artists strutting their stuff in characteristic style.

Here, for the price of a beer or two you experienced some raw singing performed to even rougher guitar accompaniment, but both served up with artistry which makes the more commercial flamenco seem tame and anaemic by comparison.

Following up on an advert in the local paper I tunnelled through the narrow streets of the old city behind the Cathedral. Failing to find any name board and relying solely on the metal number plate pinned to the wall like any other property in the street, I tried the heavy oak door. Inside was a bar also of heavy dark oak construction supporting a few small kegs of wine already tapped and ready to pour. Half a dozen tables, some round some square, and an assortment of wooden chairs filled part of the stone paved space, while to one side and facing a space at that side, were a number of other wooden chairs arranged in theatre style and waiting for a performance to begin.

There was a small gathering of what were obviously locals.

One or two musicians strummed away at guitars and maybe ten minutes or so passed before the action was properly underway.

A woman, possibly in her forties, probably carrying a pound or two more than necessary, and dressed in a far from fancy, everyday dress, took to the side "stage" along with an older man carrying a guitar.

He began to play while she sat close by waiting.

A mixture of heavy strumming beats and the plucking of his fingers produced a close to magical sound, music full of rhythm and nothing short of surprising chords.

The guitar was not only invented in Spain; Spanish music, more than any other, is made for it.

Then the woman began to sing, but sing is the wrong word. Her rich, deep guttural voice shouted out her song. Was it a song or was it a spell that pulled the listener in, dominating the senses, carrying them forward and upward to become one with the singer and the emotion she kindled?

All the time she clapped out the flamenco beat.

Flamenco clapping seems at first to be an ordinary affair, a mixture of quavers and semi-quavers and if the uninitiated join in or attempt to copy the clap this is what they inevitably do.

They should listen more closely. The beat is steady, the rhythm comes not so much from varying the timing but by simply, although that is probably the wrong word, changing the strength of the beat.

With them the music became alive. It was an art form. They were playing together as only two great musicians can.

From time to time another woman, again dressed in simple, everyday fashion would take to the floor, an improvised board - a square of wood placed on the stone, and brought in the final dimension of flamenco as she danced.

Hers was not the familiar commercial style of dance, but a wild, passionate display that sent everybody's blood racing, spirits souring.

To most outsiders, the flamenco is the dance; the singing and guitar just providing a backdrop. Here, however, was true flamenco with the guitarist, the singer and the dancer fused as one in their performance.

Flamenco is the pop music of the Seville region. Recorded flamenco dominates the music stores. The papers are full of adverts offering to teach guitar, singing or dance in flamenco style. In the athletics stadium as a Spanish competitor took centre stage in the jumps or on the track the crowd would clap with mounting excitement all in flamenco rhythm. Flamenco is in their blood, so to speak, their nature, their heritage.

So the Spanish in the small crowd drank in the music and dancing, and a real if controlled excitement urged the trio to give even more life to their performance.

The next evening I took along a couple of fellow reporters after work at the stadium had finished.

"Come and hear this," I said. "It is not to be missed."

They came along with no small feelings of trepidation having been told this was an area of the city centre to avoid at night. They entered the bar and bought a glass of wine with wary looks at what was again a largely local clientele.

Once the performance began they soon forgot all that. By the end of the set they were giving the flamenco team a standing ovation and we stayed on for another set.

This was the sort of opportunity that work brought me.

Another night in Lisbon I turned up at one of the city's fado restaurants.

Fado is and was the protest music of Portugal as the people suffered for almost five decades under the fascist, right wing regime of dictator Antonio Salazar.

It was a Monday night, (the championships I was covering had finished on the Sunday night and I had stayed on to take in something of the city). Most such establishments were closed and since it was a Monday night restaurants like this one were empty or nearly so.

This one was absolutely dead.

However, the proprietor insisted I come in and once I was into my meal laid on the floor show for me, and just me alone.

He had spent part of his life working in the USA and not surprisingly spoke English well.

Since I was on my own, he explained, he had cut the programme slightly short - not that I had noticed.

So on previous working trips to Birmingham I had discovered the Fox public house and had used it on numerous occasions.

However, not on the night in question.

It was as much as I could do to fall into bed and get some much needed sleep.

Maybe I am getting old.

14

Next morning we had early starts. I was first off in my group at 10.00 and Katharine was scheduled for 10.02.

Despite the forecast and its promise of heavy rain it was a great morning, sun shining and warm enough to make anything other than running gear unnecessary.

Brightly coloured club tents, open air sports shops staffed by orienteering specialist traders, plus a mixture of cafés and food wagons gave the morning all the atmosphere which had been missing at the wet and freezing Jan Kjellstrom.

So with a little time to spare after getting kitted out, I stroll around dropping a word here and there with old acquaintances and checking out the finish.

Then I ready myself and set out for the start.

Of course I have come already prepared with an hour or so spent looking over my old JK map and course from the area.

The pre-event information on access and parking has given me a fairly shrewd idea of where the assembly and finish field are situated. I got that spot on and as it turns out the course is shaped quite as I'd imagined.

The start is further down the hill than I expected but that said its location blissfully gives a long flat run towards the first control and it is number three before we come to the first climb. That's long enough to get into gear.

The start is strangely low key this early with very few people.

However, my time comes. I progress through the funnel one minute at a time and then I am off.

I head for the path crossing and a big rhododendron patch, intending to take it on the right and aim off for the depression and the first marker.

The two guys ahead take the left hand side of rhodies and after a brief check with the map I follow. They will be on different courses but they might lead me in.

They don't. Following from the west edge of the thicket I find a control – but the wrong one.

This brings up the third rule for life that comes from orienteering. People are social animals. Like dogs, we follow the pack. Like sheep we go with the flock. In life, there are always the people who want to be top dog, some because they believe they are right, some because, cynically, they want to capitalise on a basic human reaction. It means other people are making decisions for us taking us down paths that may lead to perdition.

In orienteering, it is not the would be leaders you have to fear, it is the follower that lurks in us all, even in would be leaders, ready to take over in a moment of doubt. Orienteering is full of moments of doubt.

I lose three minutes before going back to the rhodies and coming in again to find the control deep in a very small depression.

That was not at all what I expected and I set off for number two feeling decidedly unsettled.

Again I get pulled into following the man ahead and while I recover and lose little or nothing I am not in control. I plan to run the path on the climb to number three but when that means slight backtracking to follow it round the end of the spur, I again change my mind and head up the valley through a thick helping of underfoot grot to get "lost" at the top of the hill. I'm just not thinking straight.

So it carries on.

By number nine I have only my run to five to be pleased about. I am using the map, I am planning, orienteering, but my decision making is poor.

Here, again I change my mind. Set to follow a path to a junction and follow that path down to an obvious clearing and to another offshoot that will lead me straight to the control I suddenly decide to cut across country.

This is risky, going downhill to locate on one of several ridges – very typical English orienteering terrain. The right attack point is essential.

I end up searching the wrong ridge. That's another six minutes wasted.

The disappointing thing is that I am running really well, cruising, motoring, call it what you will but I have that easy feeling both on the flat and, surprisingly, on the climbs.

The one time I opted for a walk on a long, steepish climb I used the time profitably to work out the routes to the next few controls.

I had forgotten to take my beta blocker the night before so maybe that was the explanation.

Maybe that was why I was running so well and taking so many hills in my stride.

I am down to a quarter tablet per day now. My doctor says I am taking so little it won't be having any effect but if I am right, not taking that small amount is certainly having an effect.

I first became aware that I had a heart problem seven or eight years ago during a circuit training session. During squat thrusts, bringing my knees up to my chest set my heart racing.

Palpitations have long been dismissed in popular culture as a Victorian woman's complaint brought on by wearing tight corsets.

My mother had it and I dismissed her worries as of little importance too.

As my heart went back to normal with a few seconds rest I paid the complaint little attention.

Then it became a regular occurrence jumping from around sixty to over a hundred and twenty. Bending down to give the cat a saucer of food, for example, would bring it on. I would breathe out deeply before bending to keep the pressure on the heart to a minimum and that worked a bundle.

Strangely, when I later told doctors of the pressure connection they did not seem interested. They didn't say, "Ah that's because........" They just ignored the point.

Then one day, coming home from an event in the car, a sudden deceleration caused the seatbelt to punch hard against my chest. My heart started racing.

This time it took half an hour to get back to normal.

I decided it was time to see a doctor.

The look of amazement on her face when I reported that I had been ignoring this for months was unforgettable.

Not that much came of this visit. A hospital appointment was arranged but after a series of unrevealing tests, including a weekend with a home cardiogram, the consultant set my mind at ease by saying it was probably a benign condition which she called runners' heart.

It was a diagnosis which caused raised eyebrows amongst other doctors on my next enforced hospital visit.

The problem grew more regular starting without any particular stimulus. In retrospect I feel that the normal everyday pressure of work plus too great a coffee intake were to blame.

Then one day it just would not slow down.

After about an hour and half I got in the car and drove to the accident and emergency unit at the hospital. I was a bit wobbly on my legs as I walked from the car park and had to slow down.

Inside I was seen quickly.

The quick remedies, all designed to stimulate the vagus nerve, sucking on ice, pressing the eye balls, rubbing one side of the neck, failed to take effect.

It was time to call in the expert.

I was wired up by this time, and as the consultant told me, there were already signs of minor heart damage which could cause a heart attack if the beat could not be slowed down.

The Ozzie doctor, who was leading a couple of trainees, decided to stop my heart momentarily to allow it to resume its normal beat on start up.

He explained that the cardiogram readings showed that the normal spread of the electrical stimulus which makes the heart contract was feeding back in a loop and so giving two beats for the price of one. The problem was that the heart was not getting enough time or enough relaxation to fill with blood and send it out around the body and back to the heart itself.

They got one case of this a week on average, he said.

A drip catheter was fitted first. "Just in case it is needed," he told the trainees.

I didn't need to be told for what.

Then I was given an injection of adenosine.

Nothing happened.

He upped the dose.

The cardiogram showed a slight hesitation and then carried on – but the beat was back to normal.

I had noticed nothing. My eyes had seen yellow for a moment and I had a brief, very dull and very slight pain across my shoulders.

It is the kind of thing I get sometimes following the initial gulps of a cold beer.

Maybe I should give up drinking cold beers.

The problem was diagnosed as supra ventricular tachycardia, not a death threat if properly treated.

I was kept in hospital while they initiated me onto beta blockers and I went home with my little bottle of pills.

Little bottles of pills are something you associate with other people – usually old people.

I didn't like this. Having my own little bottle of pills, which I had to take with me, carry in my pocket, just in case, was a step in the wrong direction.

Their affect on my running was even more depressing.

Beta blockers, so called because they cut down the impulses travelling in the beta nerve group, not only slow the heart down but they make each beat less strong, pushing less blood out to the body. After and during exercise they hinder recovery, the heart slowing down too quickly before the carbon dioxide and other wastes have been cleared from the tissues.

You don't get breathless, you just run on tired, weak legs. Gentle slopes become hills and hills become mountains.

Heart beat irregularities, say the experts, are the principal cause of sudden death syndrome – the cause of most of the many distance running deaths, often in people who were not aware they had an irregularity.

I have known people who have dropped dead out running.

Statistically, I stand a one in three chance of doing exactly that.

Why then do I do it? Well, I have got to say it is a better way to go than many even if I have never been an advocate of the "he died happy doing what he wanted to do" hypothesis.

Besides, the statistics also say that I am nine times more likely to drop dead if I give up running.

I always go out with my pills – beta blockers and nitrate - in my pocket.

107

On two pills a day I was half asleep most of the time and had to hold on getting out of my car just to stop falling over.

Half a pill twice a day was workable although medical eyebrows were still raised at my already low heart rate down to forty-two beats per minute.

I was put on aspirin to "thin" my blood.

This was getting ridiculous. I could foresee a time when I would need another pill to counteract the effect of the aspirin and then another yet again to combat that one's effect.

I whittled it down further. Officially it may be ineffective at such low concentrations, but I still feel it affects my running,

Anyway, at Cannock, purely by accident, I had taken no pills within the previous 24 hours and I was running well. Maybe I was running too well. Maybe that was the problem. The running was too much fun to concentrate on the navigation.

The eleventh control was interesting. At the start there had been a notice warning that part of the wood was unexpectedly out of bounds. Organisers had been told that morning that they could not use the area because rangers had found a pair of buzzards nesting there.

I had forgotten all about this until part way along the path going in its general direction I came across the large taped off section. I knew where I was and I knew where the control was, but there was no information about how large an area was taped off. It was a toss of the coin situation. Should I go left or should I go right? Both possible routes would go down hill only to climb again. The climb on the right looked slightly less than on the left hand route which had to climb back over the spur. I went right and it worked well, the flag coming into view from the bottom of the turn-in.

Route choice was important at the twelfth control, a small depression – a hole really, a bit like the first control – in a stretch of wood. The direct route went through some dense scrub and plantation. There were two longer path routes, one to the left cutting out most of the scrubland, and one to the right which was longer still but followed more line features and gave easier underfoot running. In retrospect, most of the faster times came on the right hand route. I was fifth on the leg and that was probably where I should have finished overall had my navigation been as on the mark as my running.

Again my well done "legs" were up with the top four or five, and chances are that at most events fourth or fifth to every control would see you win but the unnecessary time lost at one, three and nine put me down in twentieth place out of the forty-six starters.

Here I was almost half way through the year and my orienteering continued to lack consistency. Near perfect runs at places like Kincraig were more than outweighed by blunders like this championship run.

[See map and course at http://www.routegadget.co.uk – Appendix 1; item (h)]

15

Speaking as a runner, I don't like hills and I don't like heather.

Heather in flower is marvellous. I love it. The Scottish hills in July or August are nothing short of wondrous to behold.

However, running through heather is something else again. Six inches deep and it is like having springs in your shoes but there is not much of that type of heather around. If it is up to your calf muscles then you have problems. Once it starts scratching the knees then as far as I'm concerned, forget about running and just concentrate on keeping upright.

There is a way to run through heather.

"Pick up your knees," one top competitor told me, adding, "You've got to train for it."

Perhaps that's my problem. Not enough heather running training.

So why am I telling you all this?

Well, a number of orienteers, I might add a large number, came into the sport from hill and mountain walking.

For many of them hills are part of the sport. Almost inevitably hills play some part in the sport because if you pile a few contours together, you have a hill. To the average mountain man or woman that is not a hill, it scarcely warrants recognition as a pimple. When they talk of hills they mean real hills.

It is not so much the height as the shape of the hill that counts. It doesn't have to be high. The question is does it have all the nooks and crannies that make for testing orienteering?

Then the dyed in the wool mountain man doesn't just want to have you climbing hills, he likes to see you climbing straight up them.

I suspect that some forget that orienteering is a running sport and are much more interested in everyone "enjoying" the climb and a good view from as many summits as they can find.

There, that's that grumble over.

There is a strong element of truth in what I say.

Martin Bagness, one of Britain's top orienteers in the 1990s, went on to be one of the best course planners in the business. He wrote that if you give a top competitor too long and too steep a hill to climb then you are giving them an advantage. They will drop to a walk and use the time to plan the course ahead. The art of planning a course is to put in climbs to test fitness but keep them short so that competitors will not be tempted to take time out from running and engage in some detailed map reading while walking.

He was not talking about me, of course. If I spend time planning I can only remember the roughest detail by the time I reach the next control. It wasn't always like that. I can remember a time when I did check out a rough line to the following control and memorise its number. Now I've forgotten it all by the time I reach the control I am running to.

It isn't just the muscles that age, the brain does too.

When I hit a straight up hill, come to that any hill, I very quickly enter the land of the knackered.

It takes me all my time to keep moving, let alone read the map.

For many years I found that tackling even the smallest climb at a run made me suffer. I would be brought to a stop by the biting, extreme pain in my left "glute".

I thought that poor circulation was to blame. It took me some time to realise that since just the one leg was affected, that it was more likely a nerve problem. I calculated that pressure on a lumbar nerve was probably to blame and that it all hinged on my running style.

At one time I suffered a chronic back problem but I thought that was long behind me, so I was loath to admit this could be the cause.

Self-structured physio – reshaping my spine by stretching out on the floor - has improved the complaint. Hills do not present the problem they once did but long or repeated climbs can still have me in agony. These days a different nerve is involved and a different part of my leg are affected.

Angela Mudge is one of the world's best mountain runners. On the British domestic scene, she expects to beat most of the men and they expect her to beat them.

She won the Women's World Championship title in 2000. She has won the British Fell Running Championship five times and the Buff International Skyline Running title twice. Her other successes include the Mount Kinabalu Climbathon in Malaysia twice and the Everest marathon.

In addition, she is a cross-country runner of note having won the UK women's championship title amongst others.

Early in her career, she was also knocking at the door of British selection in orienteering only to be disappointed.

"I started too late," she says touching on one of those controversial arguments in the sport. A number of runners have notably taken up orienteering in their late teens or even later and have been relatively successful. They condemn the attitude that they see as writing mature starters off because of "an age thing".

Mudge takes the other attitude.

"I was nineteen," she says. "That is too late. If you start orienteering when you are young, the contours jump out at you."

"I was running much faster than I could navigate."

She found that mountain racing gave her not just success that she enjoyed but the uninterrupted running under the pressure and the excitement of competition she enjoyed even more.

"I'm good at running on hills because I'm good at breaking my rhythm," she says. Another way of putting it is that she can keep her rhythm while breaking and changing her stride as she meets the bumps and dips, steams, slopes and dips that come with the rough terrain of a hills or mountain landscape. "You have to do that whether you are walking or running."

Of course she owes a lot to the training she has done to uncover her genetic potential and build on her natural advantages.

"You need a great deal of cardiovascular fitness and strong 'glutes' and calf muscles," she adds.

Angela Mudge - a mountain running great

Topping a ridge during the 18 mile/5000 feet climb Ochil 2000s race
which takes in all eleven major tops in the central Scotland range.
Mudge finished fourth overall in 2008 clocking a record of 2h 51m33s.
(Ian Nimmo)

Celebrating the start of the season in fancy dress at the Carnethy
Five Tops race near Edinburgh. (Anne Nimmo)

Mudge is another of those classy runners who says, "I don't know how I do it."

Importantly she says she is a master at running up hills because of her "climbing technique."

"I shorten my stride and try to maintain the same cadence," she says.

"I think I have quite a high knee action running on the flat but I hardly lift my knees on the hills," she adds, perhaps surprisingly, for using a high knee lift to supply drive is a common technique amongst less successful hill runners.

That isn't the only accepted wisdom she has binned.

"I bend into the gradient which you aren't meant to do. They say you should keep upright to help get the air into your lungs but bending works for me."

It could be that bending helps the blood return to her heart.

However, all these things are very far from her mind as she takes the hills in her stride.

"I don't consciously adjust anything. I just run."

Hills and heather very often go together and so it was at my next two Scottish League outings.

The first was in the middle of May in the Sidlaws just north of Dundee.

The Sidlaw Hills run for some thirty miles, east to west on the north side of the Tay estuary from Perth to just past Dundee.

It is grand walking country. As said, the most famous of its summits is Dunsinane where Shakespeare's MacBeth met his death.

The Dundee folks are more acquainted with Craigowl with its display of radio masts, lying just to the north of the city and the highest point of the range.

From that summit you can look north towards Glamis which also featured in the MacBeth play.

At Auchterhouse, the slopes onto Balkello Moor are steep. The plateau is former grouse shooting country thick with heather. The grouse eat the young heather shoots.

Fortunately the mapper had managed to find a number of holes and hollows left by old quarry workings, which make for more interesting orienteering despite being hidden in the vegetation, but for the main part it was very much a matter of getting out of the heather onto the nearest path and taking a long run to the area of the next control.

Of course, I made mistakes. A couple of route choice errors saw me going for a cross-country option rather than the path both times. How could I be so stupid?

Then this was never going to be the perfect run I was after. Even if I had spiked all the controls spot on, I was never going to run to perfection on that terrain - no rhythm, never in motoring mode. There was too much heather.

Bill from Edinburgh, at 75, always a better runner and navigator than me in his younger days, took on some of the younger vets over a course half a kilometre longer than mine, and finished well up the rankings.

Just goes to show that some folks can do it come hills or high heather.

His knees are closer to the ground than mine.

Big disappointment of the day was getting caught and dropped by an "old guy" over the last four controls.

He had lost ten minutes at one of the earlier ones so I beat him on overall time.

It was galling.

The next league run was at Banchory in the Dee Valley.

This whole area, from Banchory to Braemar as well as being scenically beautiful, is rich in superlative orienteering venues and Scolty is one of these.

In the south of the mapped area there are two summits. The higher hill to the West is well wooded with mature forestry plantation and has some very intricate contours.

The going is rough and the orienteering is tricky and testing.

Scolty Hill, to the East, famed for its annual hill race (held the day before our early June visit) is something else again.

It is treeless and largely featureless. Runners can be seen going into the control sites sometimes from a considerable distance. The route choice is usually limited: take one of the paths by way of the summit or trudge through the heather.

It is sad to struggle across this when you know that there is not far short of excellent, intricate, fast running orienteering on the flatter ground below that you will barely sample.

"Where did you go"? I asked one of the elite course runners.

"Everywhere," he replied.

His moor run was two kilometres out of ten and his legs could take it at speed but for veterans it was two out of just over five. To my way of thinking that is half the course wasted.

I was running what is called up distance: a course longer than set for my age class, so I shouldn't grumble. If I do, I don't do it officially.

Why was I running up distance, you might ask?

Well, at most events you find that each course is shared by a number of different age groups.

At Dundee, for example, I shared with runners aged thirty-five to seventy, some running their "short" age class course, usually because they are not as fit as they might be and opt for a shorter distance.

Time after time however this course is headed by the sixteen and seventeen year old girls, many of whom are knocking at the door of British youth team selection.

They have a spring in their step the likes of which I can't even remember, and a strength to weight ratio I can only dream about without becoming anorexic.

I have long since become used to losing out to both female and younger opposition.

There is a national ranking scheme in orienteering with the points standardised by the fastest on the course. These teenagers were setting standards which not only could I not match but which gave me fewer points than I could get running the slightly longer courses against other opposition.

Mind you, at Scolty, even if I had hit every control spot on I would not have been picking up ranking points, I could not in all honesty have claimed a perfect run. I ran but I ran badly right from the start. It was such heavy going.

To the first control I headed through a thick ground cover of fallen trees and brashings, as the off-cuts are called. I kept a close eye on the thick trees to the North and hit the control spot on but I had taken a long time.

The thick going continued forcing me to use a recent machine track early on the next leg.

Felling machines with their caterpillar tracks can create havoc in a woodland, and while the tracks are eroded in time they are deep and rutted to start with. I was clambering along them rather than running. To make matters worse, this one led off at an angle. The forest alternative was harder going still.

I lost my concentration and my confidence and I slowed right down into number two even although it was an easy trackside control.

The next few controls I ran well before making a basic navigation mistake at number six where despite all the evidence, I left the path too early and wasted five or more minutes running around in circles before I realised what I had done. All this was energy sapping stuff. It was slow going over the next two controls and all the while my legs were tiring still more.

Heading for nine I picked up on a forest break or "ride" a hundred metres downhill which seemed to offer faster going than the over hill route alternative but the ride produced just one bundle of fallen trees after another. There was little or no running to be found there. Then it was onto the hill and into the heather. No running for me there either.

I struggled down from the control, my spirits soaring at the sight of an extensive stretch of short, cropped grass ahead and a wide path which stretched off down to the saddle before rising towards the open summit of Scolty Hill beyond. I could follow it into the dip and then turn left onto another path and two hundred metres would take me to the next marker. I could see people running into it from where I was. This was going to be easy.

By now my legs were in no condition to make use of easy going. After all I had been through I was just not fit enough. I tried to stretch it out down the slope but each stride jarred, sending sharp, jolting vibrations up through my legs and body. It hurt.

I left the path and tried running on the grass but it was little better. I should have remembered those Kenyans at the Edinburgh cross-country, kept the knees bent, shortened my stride out front, but I wasn't thinking that way. I was scarcely thinking at all. To save my legs from what seemed certain damage I took to the heather, adopting a straight line approach.

The change stopped the pain but I was back in that tough running zone.

So it went on: ploughing through the heather to ten, then even longer heather to eleven before tumbling down through heather on my way to twelve.

Hitting the forest floor at the foot of the hill was like coming out of a torture chamber into the real world. Everything was as it ought to be, easy running, little timber litter, a place to relax in.

I ran, not where I was meant to run - a woman in walking boots and a carrying a walking stick caught me up as I circled around number thirteen - but I ran and lapped it up.

It had not been a pleasant day.

[Balkello - see map and course at http://www.routegadget.co.uk – Appendix 1; item (i)

Scolty - see map and course at http://www.routegadget.co.uk – Appendix 1 item (j))]

16

There's nothing quite like it.

As Daniel Hubmann says, to run with full control somewhere in a forest is a great feeling.

It is.

Here I am at the Scottish Champs.

I am heading for number ten, a biggish boulder half way down the slope into the next valley, and am I feeling good.

The Scottish Championships is the third of the big three - the JK, the British and then the Scottish. That is not just for me and not just for other Scots but for large numbers of British runners who like to take the opportunity of taking in some top calibre orienteering terrain.

The venue is Rannoch Forest on the south side of Loch Rannoch, one of the most remote parts of Highland Scotland, twenty miles from the A9 north/south artery.

The road ends ten miles further on at Rannoch Station and a further ten miles of moorland and forest track will take the adventurous walker through the wildest stretch of British countryside to join the Glasgow to Fort William Road close to mountainous Glencoe.

Rannoch Moor is where the last ice age started in Britain. It is high, desolate, dangerous, covered with black lochans and reputedly bottomless peat bogs.

The annual Etape Caledonia cycle trial, which attracts a British-wide entry, goes all round Loch Rannoch before heading back to Pitlochry.

The Black Wood of Rannoch, immediately to the west of our competition area is one of the few remaining, now protected areas, of the original Caledonian pine forest.

It is a rare and beautiful spot.

So as I was saying...

The long downhill to number six followed by three control picking markers virtually on the flat and my legs are feeling full of running.

This is a long up hill leg, the kind of thing that normally can take the wind from my sails as well as my lungs. However, I'm still running happy.

I pick up the pace, lifting my knees, flicking my heels, driving not hard but hard enough to keep the all important rhythm of the run going.

I'm still running happy.

What's this, three big teenage lads just ahead and they are walking. I'm pulling them in.

I saw them just moments ago on the way to number nine. They were trying to out-sprint each other as they raced for their own control nearby. Now they are paying for it.

Done it. Passed them. If I was feeling good before, now I'm feeling even better.

Now they are behind me and I'm crossing the forest track with the main bit of the climb still to come but there is no stopping me now.

I'm still running hard as I take my angle from the little quarry to my left and head off over the spur, aiming for a patch of thicker plantation, still out of sight at the moment but waiting down into the valley on the other side. I can use that as my attack point.

There's a forty-something woman ahead going well but not as well I am.

I pass her too.

There's no stopping me now.

Well, that's not true. A patch of blaeberry, very rough underfoot has me down to a slow jog but that's what I've got to do, adapt my running to the conditions.

Now I'm through it and running again and feeling so easy.

There's the thicket I'm looking for. I look for the angular, pointed end turn to the right full of expectation but there's no sign of the boulder.

Here comes that sinking feeling again.

There are a couple of people over there. Maybe they have found it. There's temptation – scoot over there and join them

Stop it. Control yourself. Use the map. They are too far over anyway.

Check the area, I tell myself.

I do.

I turn around and there it is, the boulder, and there's the kite, just behind me.

I spike it.

As I leave I notice that the other side, the side I approached, is fairly well covered with moss making the boulder itself well camouflaged and hard to see.

Oh that they had all been as spot on as that one!

My Scottish Championships did not start that well. The first control put paid to my perfect run ambitions for that day.

Standing at the start, I kept one eye on the runners going out. (They can be pointer to where you should go). I picked up on one of the top juniors who frequently runs the same course I do. He went off to the left. Ah-ha, I told myself knowingly nodding my head in appreciation of my own cleverness. When I set out minutes later I took the same line.

Of course, I was jumping to conclusions – again. He was on a different course and heading for a nearby track. When I finally got round to taking a close look at my map and lining it up with my compass I see that I have gone off ninety degrees to the left. Something inside me started to cry.

The sensible thing to do was to go back to the start kite and begin again......begin again with at least three minutes thrown away. I did just that.

As controls go, number one, just two hundred metres away, was a real stinger in any case and I lost more time before finding it.

The next two tricky controls I picked up in short order. I was into my stride, picking my way around and between the blaeberry covered hummocks and my mistake was forgotten as I set out south west on a long seven hundred metre leg that took in a couple of big spurs and a valley lined at the bottom with a belt of thicker trees.

There was a gap through the trees which would lead to a major tree thicket up the next slope. It would be my attack point. The little valley I was after was just around the corner from there.

Instead of climbing along the straight route, I swung round to the left to avoid the summits and take in the tree belt from the slope above to find the gap.

I found it, or I thought I had. Down I went and through the other side. There was something wrong. The thicket was on my left. It was meant to be on my right. I had to check it out just in case there was another unmapped gap past mine. I ran up to where the control might have been before deciding that I had indeed found an unmapped gap but one that meant I had crossed the valley bottom too soon. I had failed to make use of a tree thicket standing out like a sore thumb just before making my crossing. It was on the map. It should have set me up to use the gap and then turn right.

I ran on along the side of the valley, found the thicket and the control and was back on course. In years gone by a check-out like this might have cost me a minute or so. Now? Well, four extra minutes had gone up in smoke.

Close by, number five and then six – another long run back over the hill - were again spot on although I lost time dithering on the long down slope to six. It was shapeless, lacking in features other than waffly clumps of trees.

Boosted by my great run to ten I picked off the last four controls with a few minor route adjustment to contend with the vegetation on the way, pushing hard while keeping on the sensible side of anaerobia and maintaining the rhythm.

The last small, steep slope from the river crossing and into the finish field emptied what was left in my legs and I could scarcely raise a canter let alone a sprint on the run in.

I just failed to break the hour, 61m15s, was eighteenth out of close to a hundred starters on my course, the first of the veteran men and Scottish age group Champion.

Just two mistakes, but two mistakes that had lost me maybe ten places.

On the other hand, much class "A" running had saved the day.

[See map and course at http://www.routegadget.co.uk – Appendix 1; item (k)]

17

Sixty minutes of undiluted running pleasure.

It is the middle of June and the last big event of the early season is at Culbin on the Scotland's Moray coast near the small town of Forres.

This was the venue for the World Championship Relays away back in 1976.

Along with the individual championships staged at nearby Darnaway, this was the first time the "Worlds" were held in Britain and they proved to be a take off point for orienteering in the country.

Olympic steeplechase medallist Chris Brasher, who graduated into journalism after his life on the track and before going on to take a leading role in the London Marathon, was a leading light in the sport in England then.

He took on the mantle of British orienteering's press officer for the championships and used his connections to ensure not only a strong press presence at the championships but in-depth TV coverage by the BBC into the bargain.

Remember these were the days when TV sport meant just that and not TV football. Saturday afternoon coverage then could include up to half a dozen different sports.

The championships did not get a Saturday afternoon slot, but a composite piece put out on BBC2 one evening midweek attracted a huge audience.

The result was that orienteering blossomed and took off.

The large veteran fields at most British events today go back to this era when a host of people, some already involved in sports like athletics, but many more who found in orienteering a competitive sporting niche, took up the sport.

Culbin is a forested area of sand dunes, some over a hundred feet high.

Once it was a major Highland farming area with settlements and villages as well as a big country estate.

However, at the end of the seventeenth century a number of sand storms, including the Great Sand Drift of 1694 saw the area overwhelmed by deposits from the neighbouring beach.

One village was taken out, covered over and buried, in just one night.

Extensive tree planting initiated some 150 years ago helped to stabilise the dunes but it was not until a Forestry Commission project, started in the 1920s, planted nine thousand acres of trees, largely Scots pine, that the threat of the drifting sands was finally halted.

The result is one of the best orienteering areas in the country.

Twisting lines of dunes are separated by flats covered with soft, bouncy lichens. Fresh growths of conifers, some thicker plantations, and spreading areas of birch close down the visibility in places lending to the variety and making navigation more difficult.

So the Culbin orienteering recipe takes competitors to the edge.

There is much fast running. The temptation is always to go too fast, that means too fast to navigate.

The terrain mixture is demanding.

There is open, flat and rolling dune forest where accurate location is difficult bordering on impossible once "lost".

At the 2009 British Championships I was lost for over twenty minutes on a fifteen hundred metre leg. I misread the bends on a road I was crossing and went onto the wrong hill in the forest.

Going onto the wrong hill as I did then is known as a parallel feature error. That means you mistake a feature on the map for a nearby similar feature on the ground.

It is a common mistake at all levels in the sport. I remember a former British number one who ruined his World Championship final at the first control when he ran onto the wrong ridge.

There are areas of complex hollows and small hills, sometimes with a mix of dense and not-so-dense vegetation, that bring all but the very best map readers down to a walk if they want to keep in contact and know exactly where they are.

Probably the best "off road" running in the world - Culbin Forest on Scotland's Moray Coast

Control 62 Culbin (Malcolm Aldridge)

Following the ridge (Malcolm Aldridge)

So from the start, off I go, off the forest road start and right into the trees..... trees with heather underfoot, a rarity in these parts. Fortunately the undergrowth is long and straggly, easily brushed aside and easy running compared with the heather terrain on some recent outings. Over the "ride" and into easy running territory I'm about half way there, and the ridge I want lies right ahead. The dune I am after is the second one of two about sixty meters further on. My line has been more or less perfect.

This is orienteering running at its best.

The next four controls go by – another knoll, then a valley cunningly hidden in some thicker plantation, and then a path run around an area of young, really dense forest to another knoll just over the summit of a seriously large dune – and this has all the makings of a perfect run. I'm using the map, picking my control features and attack points.

I'm navigating and running well. This is a gem.

OK, keep it up, let's get number five, one of a clutter of small knolls on a ridge about three hundred metres away. This could prove tricky.

I set off on compass but run into problems with some of the shapes. I change my plan, simplifying the terrain, and now I am looking for a big area of flat ground the other side of a really big spur. That will be my attack feature. I go on rough compass and cross the spur but there is no sign of the flat area. Maybe it just looks flatter on the map than on the ground.

I hit a ride and feel that first spur of panic. There was no ride on my route plan. I stop. It's time to take an eyes down, concentrated look at my map and narrow in on the alternatives. There's just one possibility. It lies off my intended line to the right.

I line up the map to fit, check with my compass, relocate and then race on to the ridge which is still some a hundred and fifty metres away. After a brief pause there I hit the control.

This is what orienteering is all about; recovering from mistakes quickly and carrying on.

This mistake will prove to have cost me over two minutes. How time flies when you are thinking.

Orienteering, more than most sports, lends itself to analysis with splits – times between the controls - and maps available on the internet. One website allows downloading of the map and courses so that you can mark up the route you took and see what alternatives worked or failed to work for the opposition.

The next four controls twist the course round on itself but I pick them off with little trouble apart from losing ten-seconds misreading number nine on a little ridge close to a thicket.

The next four are in a loop in the opposite direction on another dune complex three hundred metres further on and across the forest road.

None of them are easy and tiny mistakes are beginning to add up.

All of them need map work and a deal of thinking to translate it to the ground.

Then it's a long path run with a classical right-left route choice. I go right. My legs are beginning to feel the strain. The path is sandy and gives little grip even with studs.

I try to ignore it while throttling back a fraction. Maybe the left route would have been firmer but there was nothing on the map to show that. It would certainly have given a better attack point and I have a moment's apprehension before striking out across the final two hundred metres of forest.

Skirting an area of young trees I can see a line of pines ahead. That's what I want, the north-east corner of this vegetation change. Only four more controls to go.

I hit the next path. A left turn along it will give me a one hundred meter run until I reach a thicket on the left – the perfect attack point. Turn there and run another hundred with a big patch of young conifers on my left and I will nail it – a knoll with the marker perched on its south east corner.

Then I reasoned, the patch of young trees could act as the attack point for a head-on attack. I went for it. I had no real reason to go for broke. It was blatant arrogance to do so.

The problem was there were other young trees around from a lot of self planting in the area. While most trees in a plantation are man planted, increasingly saplings that have grown from seed dropped by the surrounding trees are being left to grow. They make for interesting orienteering, pushing up thickets all over the place.

It is one of these which unwittingly I have my eye on. I get there to find – nothing. I get pulled off by another clump to the right before taking control and heading back to the track.

Everything is more difficult too because of recent forestry workings.

My hope is I'll see the knoll on the way but the ground is throwing up many very minor hills, all too small to be on the map.

I hit the track, locate the real patch of young trees and head back in.

I find the knoll but it was not an easy control.

Those forest machines had carved up the ground around it. It was obviously going to be harder going from here on, both for running and navigation.

So it proved, with thick, nebulous vegetation masking number seventeen and the route to eighteen. I lost time at both.

I finished up eighth in a forty-plus strong field and was second of the old men – by just nine-seconds. The annoying thing is I could have been first of the old men but for that mistake at five or the foul up at sixteen.

Although the final five hundred metres left a nasty taste they did little to detract from what had been a first class day. Run in Culbin and barring disaster, you finish smiling.

This is what orienteering is all about. This is what running should be all about, cruising this way and then that through the trees, soft and easy underfoot, going up hill and down but all in your stride, the smell of the conifers, the sun shining – runner's heaven.

[See map and course at http://www.routegadget.co.uk – Appendix 1; item (l)]

18

It had been fairly hectic going since March travelling here and there knocking up close to a thousand miles in the car. Despite a two week break in Poland, I had been to something like fifteen events big and small, and in June alone, with the final weekend to go, I had already notched up over twelve hours training, one and a half hours in competition, a further eleven hours walking the hills plus a 9km trail race.

I felt fitter. I had even put in a couple of double session days. My technique was improving, becoming more consistent even under pressure.

Next up, June twenty-seventh, was the final event of the spring season, the last event before the summer break which surely presented a last chance to capitalise on all that had gone before with a perfect run.

As far as I am aware, Britain is the only European country to have a split orienteering season.

Portugal and Spain have winter seasons staging their top events from January through to March and avoiding the soaring summer temperatures which make long distance running a nightmare.

Most of the others adopt the Scandinavian model.

These northern neighbours have a strong domestic and international winter season in ski orienteering, reverting to foot orienteering when the snows clear in March.

Their foot-O season then runs through to September, finishing more or less, with the national championships.

However, in Britain the season stops during the summer.

This has got nothing to do with soaring temperatures.

First, fewer people are around to take part in what is to some extent, a family sport. When the schools break up and folks go away on holiday, numbers can fall off to the point where the turnout at local events often makes them not worth organising.

Even more to blame is British ecology. Many British woods and forests used in orienteering are deciduous and the wetter British summers produce a meteoric rise in undergrowth including nettles and brambles which make running far from pleasant.

Almost everywhere, woods and hillsides are plagued by bracken which breaks through in May but can reach head high and higher by July.

Bracken is the fern which has branching fronds. You can swim through it when it is young, using a kind of stand up breaststroke to part the fronds with your arms.

As it grows, this devilish cunning plant, has its fronds intertwine and knit together, causing an almost impenetrable barrier.

It grows highest in the dips and valleys so the contour shapes, the curves and slopes so essential to navigation, are first smoothed out then disappear all together. At the same time it hides the rocks, smaller crags and holes underfoot. So many of the potential control sites are hidden. That's not only bad for orienteering it is positively dangerous with hidden holes and rocks waiting there to trip even the most wary.

Bracken won't grow at altitude, and it is either absent or poorly developed in heather, on very thin dry soils and in marshy land. So sometimes and only sometimes, it is possible to pick your way to avoid the worst of it.

It is found across the world but in many areas of Europe it is relatively scarce.

Not so in Britain where it is regarded as a major pest.

Some years ago, a scientist working in the field of bracken control told me that the best way to get rid of bracken was to plant trees; that it was a light loving plant which preferred the open hills and woodland clearings.

That is certainly so, but with all the ingenuity that nature has at its disposal, it appears to have adapted since then. Increasingly, apparently dark adapted varieties are extending their domain into all but the darkest woods or areas where the competition from other ground level plants is more than they can handle.

The British spring season starts in January or February although until mild winters became the fashion in recent years, the season, especially outwith southern England, might not get under way until March. Orienteers living in the North were at a definite disadvantage when it came to the JK and British Champs because their southern neighbours had much more serious competition behind them by the time these events came along.

After the summer break, the autumn series gets under way in September and runs through until late November.

So two weeks after our trip to the Moray coast here we are on Deeside in Aberdeenshire where the local club was holding an open event in Sluie woods at Potarch for this last event of importance on the early season calendar.

Potarch is a charming and popular picnic spot just off the A93, the road which runs from Aberdeen, through Braemar and over the southern Grampian Mountains at the Glenshee ski resort towards Perth and the Scottish midland conurbations.

An open green, surrounded by woods stands at the road junction overlooked by a quaint, stone built, traditionally Scottish style hotel dating back to the eighteenth century.

The River Dee, good for paddling and occasional swimming, runs between the green and the main road.

There are children playing in the water as we arrive and head across the bridge and the main road into the woods for the competition.

It's hot, humid, and one of those days that seem to lack air.

Worse still, my ankles have not recovered from my club run on Thursday and warming up has done nothing to iron away the niggles and pains. So much for any chance of a good run.

My idea is to concentrate on navigation technique.

Mousing through a coaching forum on an "O" internet website I came across a novel tip. It was an easily remembered acronym for one approach ..... CASH.

The C stands for Control: look at the site on the map and control list; know what you are looking for and build a picture in your head. Verbalise it if it helps. There is no time to spare on this crucial move. Able, experienced runners do it in an instant. The best will have done it on the way to the control they have just spiked.

The A stands for attack point, any more easily located feature close to the control. The plan is find it and attack the control site from there.

The S stands for "stopper", any feature the far side of the control feature which will stop you if you have missed it.

In top grade competition a stopper may be hard to find and a subtle change in the contours may be the best available. On the other hand, pacing in from the attack point, possibly at a walk, to measure the distance may be the only stopper on offer. "It's around here. I've gone far enough."

Finally, the H stands for handrail, in short the feature or series of features you can follow to your attack point. This may include the obvious: paths, fences, the edges of woods and clearings, and in many cases a good series of features, especially any that make for easy running, will determine which attack point you will use.

Again in higher level competition, the hand rails are likely to be a series of contour features, hills, ridges, valleys, slopes, depressions. At some point between you and the next control the only handrail available will be your compass.

Well, that's the idea, I go out with CASH in mind, and for the first two controls it has worked well enough.

On the way to number three the bracken is thicker and likely to hide the boulder I'm looking for. I am on a compass bearing as the features begin to get swamped by the vegetation and heading for a small hill two hundred metres away which looks a first rate attack point.

I hit it (or so I thought), change my bearing and go for the control.

There is no boulder or kite to be seen. Are they both hidden in the bracken? This could mean I've wandered off my bearing, or more likely, I have been forced off by the bracken.

I back pedal, pick up my previous line and carry on. Sadly my technique is already breaking down for I have forgotten to pace count and have no stopper in mind.

By good fortune I find one, a ride running east to west across much of the map. I relocate, turn round and head for the now easily seen kite hanging head high from a tree. The boulder is beneath it.

On the way to four, the bracken is getting thicker but it reaches all time stopper quality around number seven.

I am in deep trouble by that time, after a series of beginner standard blunders.

Standing despondent on a softly rolling slope with the bracken drowning the contours I am lost. Relocation is well nigh impossible.

After fifteen minutes stumbling around I am on the point of jacking it in.

Two things stop me. I know from experience that dropping out leaves a nasty aftertaste. As I stand there on the hillside looking in the direction of home I face a deep sea of bracken reaching as far as I can see. The forest road is down there somewhere but where? I need to find the control to know where I am and find my way home. So, I tell myself, I might as well go on.

A couple of years ago this area was used for a big early autumn event. The relatively small areas of bracken which grew there then are marked on the map. How it has spread! There is no way it could be used for a major event now.

Just then a couple of others hove into view. The young guy says he has been at this control before earlier on his course (it has been used twice) but he still can't find it now.

We search around and all of sudden as I wander up the slope, the map begins to fit. There are too many contour features here. We are too high. I relocate my position on the map and set off down the slope on a rough bearing until slowly, the long lost knoll we are looking for emerges like a rising wreck from the sea of vegetation.

I give the others a shout and head in to spike it.

So it is off down the hill in a relatively bracken free direction.

A couple of sixteen year olds, a boy and girl, who had followed me into the control go by running and jumping and whooping for joy while I pick my way, stumble and occasionally slither down behind them.

Why? Why can't my legs run like that, why can't I have the confidence to launch myself willy-nilly into the great unknown? Two years ago an eleven year old lad skipped by me as I struggled in rocky underfoot going and that was on the level.

My deteriorating nerve supply is probably partly to blame.

My ankles are shot to pieces now.

Normally, the proprioceptors, the nerves in the joints which relay information on position and movement to the brain, have the muscles adjusting for both movement and balance in diminutive fractions of a second or at least they should do.

Some time ago now, my physio asked me to stand on one leg. I could do it but not for long, and the ankle was shaking and twisting like a wobble board all the time. The other was not much better.

Just to make her point she stood there on one leg without a tremor. Years of running on hard ground and rough ground have taken their toll. The theory is that the nerves get damaged. When it comes to running on rough ground now I am at a distinct disadvantage.

That is only part of the story. I have also lost the bounce and spring I once accepted as normal. The main cause of this is muscle changes that have caused them to lose their elasticity.

Once like rubber balls, now they are more like dough balls.

The muscles, just like the heart, contain the elastic molecule titin and have elastic protein built into the tissues which surround the fibres and no doubt elasticity is lost from both of these with passing time.

The main problem appears to be the build up of collagen - the face cream marketer's favourite protein.

Collagen, which incidentally you can rub onto your skin but not into it, makes up the packing tissue in the muscles, the muscle sheath and the tendons which pass on the muscle pull on to the bones to cause movement.

This collagen increases throughout life but is more than matched by the proportion of muscle fibre that is built up during early adult years.

As time goes by the high collagen content out balances the fibres and the muscles become stiffer, less mobile, less powerful.

So there is a loss in strength as well, aggravated by a reduction in muscle fibre tissue, especially the powerful fast twitch fibres. The old suffer a marked reduction in power as well as strength.

This is not just a couch potato syndrome. It is an almost universal result of ageing. It happens in flatworms.

It can be slowed down and even reversed however by exercise, and while endurance running can play its part, high resistance exercise such as weight training are particularly useful at increasing muscle fibre content.

One authority advises at least two such sessions a week, advocating eight or so sets of six repetitions. They say you have to work at it using at least seventy percent of your maximum and more if you can manage it.

The overall affect of the muscle breakdown doesn't just take the wolf-like spring from your step. It means you have to step over obstacles you once would jump; it makes your stride shorter; it slows you down.

Nowadays I am almost as slow going downhill as up.

By the time I reach the bottom of the hill, the kids are out of sight and long since gone.

From then on it is a mixture of bracken and just plain, no frills, hard going. My splits will show that for most of the controls I am up with the others in the class but my disaster at number seven leaves me well down the field, creeping just inside a hundred minutes for just under six kilometres.

It was a depressing way to finish the spring season for close to everything that could have gone wrong for me had gone wrong, including my running.

[See map and course at: http://www.routegadget.co.uk – Appendix 1; item (m)]

19

So its summer time and British orienteering is over.

Not surprisingly the real sporting fanatic doesn't just sit back and accept this major set back to their enjoying life to the full.

They get up, pack their bags and head for continental Europe where the season is in top gear with a growing number of five or six day events to choose from.

Multi day events are more or less the prerogative of orienteering as far as running sports are concerned. Road racing has dabbled with them but somehow they have never really taken off at the mass participation level.

That's strange given that most road runners are out every day and while they will be training at below racing pace there is no reason why they can't race a multi day event at below full racing pace or their usual racing distance.

One summer I wrote regularly on a distance runner who turned accepted wisdom on its head by racing a half marathon almost every weekend of the season, and winning them as well.

Coaches and other competitors shook their heads in disbelief and none if any followed his example.

Orienteering multi day courses are slightly shorter than normal, and now there is an increasing use of both sprint and middle distance being incorporated into the event programme.

Many will run below maximum speed although I can't remember doing so.

I find it is more a case of running as fast as I can on increasingly slower legs.

Not uncommonly a rest day midway gives some chance to recover.

The biggy in multi day events is the O-Ringen.

This Swedish Five Day, staged in the second last week in July, is the most prestigious of them all.

It not only attracts club runners from all over the world, it also pulls in the best runners in the world to its elite field.

In its heyday during the 1980s it would have had 25,000 runners going out on each of the five days, a total of 125,000 runs, which gave it good reason to claim the status of being the "biggest mass participation sports event in the world". Even the London and New York marathons don't compare.

These days it can still expect a 15,000 strong entry, many attracted by its reputation for providing world class international opposition across the age groups, others by the feeling that any orienteer worth their salt has to be there at least once in their competitive lifetime and enjoy the circus of the best open, participatory sporting event in the world.

I've done it – been there.

Back in the 80s and 90s the European Tour was popular, with people doing a circuit of several multi events in different countries but for one reason or another we always missed out.

So a couple of years ago we decided to make up for lost time and I put together a six week circuit that took in four multi day events and five countries, travelling by bus and train.

We started in Poland competing at the Wawel Cup three day event in the countryside around the splendid city of Krakow. A weekend fixture, laid on by one of the local clubs, would not normally be financially viable, but by using it as the starting point for our tour it became very much a good opener giving us another chance to enjoy the excellent Polish terrain and maps.

From there we journeyed by train through eastern Slovakia, stopping off in Kosice overnight, on our way to the Hungarian Cup five day event in Tata close to Budapest.

We needed a rest after that one so we took a break visiting Bratislava and heading north for a few days walking near Trencin in Slovakia.

Surprisingly, this little town is very much a hub for many of the trans-Europe buses. It was strange to drop in on the tiny, old fashioned bus station of an evening and see a coach with LONDON on the destination board.

Then we moved on by bus to Olomouc in the Czech Republic to run over six days in the spectator events at the World Championships.

Often, that first hour or so when you get off a bus on the outskirts of a large town are hectic as you scrabble to find your bearings and come to terms with the local transport. Not unusually, as this time, some helpful citizen will step forward to assist in halting or non-existent English, and, as then, others on the tram will advise where we should get off. It all seems so strange at first but by the time you leave it has all become so familiar.

From there, after taking in the German cities of Dresden and Leipzig, we joined up with five hundred or so other multi nationals, for five days of sun, cakes, coffee, good fun and high quality running at the small German five day event staged by the Uslar club near Gottingen.

One attraction of this type of competition centred holiday is that it gives more opportunity to meet with other people compared with the run of the mill tourist jaunt. Even if you can't speak their language too well, when everyone is in the same group, there is more of an element of camaraderie, everyone mixing and joining in.

This year, we cut our tour to just one event. It was back to the Hungarian Cup.

One of the attractions of eastern European countries is that it costs less for accommodation, eating out, and competition fees than in Scandinavia for example, or France, or Germany, and certainly in Britain.

We teamed up with our friends the Woodwards from our old club in Ayrshire. We had done a Norwegian multi day with Charlie and Trish previously. We knew we would hit it off.

This time we started by flying into the Slovakian capital Bratislava – a city break type of location on the Danube. It has much of the atmosphere of Prague without the crowds – attractive buildings, castle, city squares, festivities, colour, people, pavement cafés, street musicians, concerts, sun and high temperatures. It was once the capital of the Austro-Hungarian Empire.

138

With temperatures around thirty-five degrees we strolled by the river, sat in the shade, enjoyed coffees and drinks, soaked in the atmosphere.

We finished the night in one of the music pubs dancing to an electric cello and guitar trio singing a spectrum of older pops which culminated with everybody up and dancing to a fifties and sixties medley.

I toyed with the idea of writing up the session in my training diary but decided that ten minutes activity on the dance floor didn't make the mark, however frantic.

Next day we split from the Woodwards who went cruising up the river for a few days in Vienna while we picked up a hired car and headed for the Ferto/Neusiedlersee area – a large nature park just to the South.

This thirty-nine kilometre long salt water lake, plus a number of other smaller lakes to the East, along with thousands of acres of agricultural land and seasonal wetland is shared by both Austria and Hungary. It is rich in bird life.

This was supposedly an iron curtain hotspot in days gone by.

A morning drive by the Austro-Hungarian border in a futile search for great bustards took us to the Andau Bridge, now a memorial to the thousands of Hungarians who crossed to the "West" at this very point during the 1956 uprising against Soviet Union control. The Soviets, who had, of course, suffered at Hungarian hands just a dozen years before during World War 2, were quite brutal in their bid to keep the country onside.

At Andau, a new wooden bridge, maybe a couple of metres wide, straddles the drainage canal. A new watch tower and a more distant old one, along with a preserved stretch of high, rusted barbed wire fencing conjure up images of the now defunct physical barrier that separated East and West Europe in days gone by. I remember such from a 1980s visit to a border crossing further south. Then it stretched off north and south into the distance. The real iron of the iron curtain.

Of course, the "West" welcomed the Hungarian influx in 1956 but the cynic in me feels that that was only because it was politically advantageous to do so, a propaganda coup.

I recollect that as East-West travel expanded, I met a Latvian who was managing his national team at a major orienteering event in Britain.

It was his first such visit so I asked him why he had not come before.

"It was too difficult," he told me pointing out that travel restrictions had made such journeys almost impossible.

"We had to travel all the way to Moscow to get permission and the chances were it would be refused," he said.

Maybe, like you now, I was thinking – "bloody Russians" - when he went on to say, "It wasn't just the travel, you had to get the visa application forms in person and then take them back again to the embassy. It would have meant queuing for many hours and even days."

Slowly, it dawned on me. If he was trying to get a visa it had to be a British visa and it was the British embassy he was talking about, the British embassy he would have had to visit in person.

He confirmed my suspicion.

It wasn't a matter of the Soviets keeping them in, as we were told. It was the British who were keeping them out, and that we weren't told.

No doubt they were all regarded as potential spies or potential asylum "scroungers".

The Vietnamese boat people found the same thing as they left post war Vietnam to evade expected retribution or a socialist life style only to find themselves imprisoned for months in Hong Kong before being shipped home.

For all their fine words and incantations of freedom, the grey suits in charge in the West did not want them.

Interestingly, while I was reporting on the European Badminton Championships in Bulgaria during the 90s I was walking in the diplomatic sector of the capital Sophia when I came across long queues of hopeful emigrants outside a number of embassies. Some, newly emerged with their application forms, were queuing up at pavement tables staffed by freelance secretaries sitting at typewriters, to have the forms filled in.

No doubt they would return to the embassy queues to submit the forms and wait for their more than likely rejection.

Relatively few if any Bulgarians were allowed in to work in Britain and other western European countries at this time.

For such people, such things had not changed over the previous decade.

It is interesting how little things can take you back over the years, spark memories.

Standing on the bridge at Andau, I recollected sitting as a fresh faced teenager in our local café drinking a bottle of coke and getting decidedly heated over Soviet military action in the streets of Budapest during the 1956 uprising, and heated too over the lack of action on Britain's part to intervene and do something about it. We would certainly have risked World War 3 and a nuclear winter.

We were too young to realise that that was not the way with politicians. Although they talked a lot, they were too involved in military colonial enterprises of their own to interrupt the Soviets in theirs.

Britain had been battling against the freedom fighters in Malaysia for eight years at the time, and was four years into a programme of harsh reprisals against the Mao Mao independence uprising in Kenya. Both bids to keep the British Empire intact were doomed to failure.

The government was still reeling from the failure and humiliation suffered in its recent attack on Egypt in a misguided bid to win back Western control of the Suez Canal with some good old gunboat diplomacy.

I can remember getting quite heated about that too over another bottle of coke.

The Andau Bridge crosses the main drainage canal which controls water levels in much of the nature reserve, one which gets little recognition internationally.

But we saw thousands of greylag geese, great white ibis by the hundred, spoonbills, plovers, sand pipers, avocets, the fragile looking black winged stilt, black redstarts, red shrike, numerous marsh harriers, hen and montague harriers, grey herons and their pack hunting relation the purple heron, and once very briefly, off in the distance following a chance look through the field glasses, a white tailed eagle.

A drive north took us to a sand quarry close to Weiden am See where the quaint bee eater nests in numbers in holes in the vertical wall.

In short, it was the proverbial bird watcher's paradise and an insight into how they are carrying out nature conservation in these parts.

We spent a morning paddling a canoe through the massive reed beds in the Hungarian part of the lake. These give the reserve its unique structure as a habitat and make it famous with those working in the field of nature conservation.

It was a guided tour which was spoiled only by the fact that the ranger spoke only Hungarian.

The going was rough by my standards when we hit open water and the whole trip proved physically testing; it certainly warranted a place in the training diary.

Then it was time to move on. With the air-con in the car working overtime, and with the high temperatures, busily breeding thunder storms, soaring again into the middle thirties, we headed for the Bakony Mountains and the Hungarian Cup.

Hungary is a country of great plains, flat landscapes that stretch to the horizon, but it is also a country of hills and mountains which stand out all the more strongly in their surroundings.

The Bakony Mountains, just to the north of Lake Balaton, are a range of rolling, tree covered hills which run for seventy miles. The highest summit is Korishegy at 706m. It stands on the Hungarian stretch of the E4 European long distance footpath. This starts on the Austrian border and goes through a series of uplands for all of 1128 kilometres before crossing the Slovakian border in the North East of the country. It is called the Blue Tour or Kektura for its marking poles carry a blue stripe between two white ones.

We had booked a room in a guest house cum restaurant or "vendeghaz" in Csesznek, a village of a few hundred people, famous for its picturesque castle.

There aremanys in Hungary.

We arrived there just in time to meet Trish and Charlie for lunch and then drove the ten or so kilometres over to the event centre to sign in, pick up our racing numbers and start times and pay our entry dues.

The exchange rate makes orienteering in Hungary a cheap option, so cheap that paying the money transfer charges can cost more than the entry fees.

142

Nobody likes paying bankers so both times out on our visits for the Hungarian Cup, I have arranged to pay our entries on arrival and cut out the money grabbing middle men.

The centre, with its impromptu camp site, was set up in one of a cluster of wooden built holiday lodges a kilometre or so from the railway station in the tiny village of Vinye. Korishegy was somewhere close to the South West but was hidden by the foothills we were to run in.

Unlike many multi day events, all the competition areas were to be within walking distance of the centre. The idea was to cut travelling to a minimum, but walks of two to three kilometres were involved. Once upon a time I would have objected to this but now I welcome the opportunity it gives to get in a "warmup".

Organisation over we were left with plenty of time to have a training run with a map in the forest, so with temperatures again in the upper thirties we headed off to the woods and the shade they had on offer.

The Bakony are constructed of limestone. Limestone usually means that there is little or no surface water to be found and apart from the river which ran through the assembly area this was true here too.

The hills were dissected by big, dry valleys which split into a number of branching fingers adding an edge to route choice and relocation.

The sides were steep and maybe twenty-five metres high making for tough running.

The forest, recognised internationally for its unique nature ecologically, was nothing short of magnificent with oak, ash, hornbeam, beach and lime all present in abundance. We don't have anything like it in Britain, or at least nothing so extensive. A carpet of fallen leaves made for soft, but energy sapping going underfoot in places, while the limestone soil was typically stony elsewhere so the feet and ankles were always under pressure, working hard to grip and find balance.

It was good running but not easy running, not super-fast.

The website had warned us that there would be nettles and there were, but little compared with deciduous woods at home.

There were many young, naturally seeded trees in patches across the forest floor. Again they made the running tougher in places, while in others they were over head height producing

143

areas of low visibility "fight" which would test both stamina and navigation.

We don't have forests like this. We all agreed this was going to be scintillating orienteering.

20

So there we were – all ready to go, all ready for five days of competition which would see me, come Sunday, standing nervously in a quiet, rain soaked forest waiting for the off signal and the start of a run which might - or might not - take me to my best ever result.

How did I get there? Well, it wasn't always easy and it wasn't always certain.

It all started on the Wednesday when we were up and off early.

Breakfast at the Erzsebet Vendeghaz, or guest house, had looked as if it might be a bit of a problem. Our landlady was less than pleasant, a bit dour and hard faced. No doubt, she felt under pressure dealing with people who could not speak Hungarian while she and her husband spoke no English, and like us had little German.

These days, however, with the Iraq War still likely to raise hackles, I have got to ask if any animosity we meet is because we are British.

This was not likely the case in question for they could have ignored our emails or hung up the phone as others in the area had done in response to my enquiries.

The next day they brought in an English speaking friend to ask us a few questions about what we wanted, and to explain about the drinks and meals available.

We booked one of her special oven baked ham dinners for the Saturday evening, both for us and the Woodwards. She smiled a bit more after that.

That first day breakfast was duly served up in time for us to make the deadline we had set, however.

At the event centre, it was already hot when we parked the car and walked to the assembly area. Wise thinking by the organisers had put this under the trees so we were spared the baking effect of the sun.

The competitions were split with medium distance events on Days 1 and 3, long events on Days 2 and 4 and a less than full length long event on Day 5 – a chasing start finale.

So there we were on day one with a medium distance run – that means not many kilometres but many controls. If all goes well that also means a quick, fast run and back within half an hour.

It was a long, hot walk to the start – uphill. The forest to the south of the assembly, a vast semicircle, had been split into five pieces so that each day we could compete in a new and different segment. The idea behind the long walk was two fold. Not only did it take us out to a new patch of forest, it also climbed out of the river valley to the plateau above and so cut down the volume of climb on the actual courses. That is an important factor when dealing with the very young and the older competitors.

On this type of terrain, the younger guys – anyone under forty – were in for a long, switch back run. They faced testing times.

I was feeling nervous. My legs felt dead even when I was walking on the flat. I knew this was all in my mind. There was no physiological reason for my legs to be dead other than the effects of too much excitement and high levels of stress hormones.

A long stretch of forest road without any shade made for really heavy going.

All I could do was hope that this would pass in my "warm up" or at the very least, once I got going.

A water wagon was available just short of the start. If water is important both for survival and to keep running at your best in long distance road or track racing, in orienteering that is doubly so.

It is said that the brain is the first organ to feel the effects of water depletion and clear thinking the first function to suffer. Many elite orienteers carry a "camel bag" of water strapped on their backs when they compete in high temperatures. A tube from the bag can be sucked from time to time to keep the body fluid level as close to normal as possible.

146

I drank some water, poured some down the back of my head and neck – very cooling – and took another cup up the last hundred metres or so to the start area, which was, thankfully, in the trees.

It is essential to check out the start at any competition, but when running abroad it is even more so for different countries can have different ways of doing things.

Control descriptions lists were available before the start. I picked one up and checked out the symbols - nothing strange.

The maps were hanging from nails in the Minus One Box. The clock was reading start time – three minutes ahead of real time. When my start time came up I would go into the box with still three minutes to go before I started.

I used up my water and tried a few up hill runs,

My legs felt better. I had a bit of a spring in my step. I tried a few more. I was feeling ready for action.

I looked around the others waiting there and noticed a guy with number 675. Mine was 676. Chances were he was on my course. I checked out the start list. There was one man due to go out after me number 677 Gyorgy Varga. Yes, number 675 Dezso Nagy was due to go out three minutes before me. I went over, pointed to my number, shook his hand and wished him good luck. He seemed an amiable fella.

I watched as he took off.

It was an uphill start. He was not going fast. Surely I could pull him in, I told myself.

However, I was three controls from home before I did.

As I ran in to number eight, a small re-entrant on the side of a spur, he was coming towards me. We had used different attack points.

Does this mean he was running faster once he got going or I am running slower than I like to think, I questioned.

So far it had been a first rate run, the closest to perfection I'd had in a long time.

I have had two minor mistakes. On the way to number two, round the edge of the plateau to the third arm of a not so dry valley, I was walking when I should and could have been running. Pick it up, I reminded myself and ran on to pick up the marker spot on. That was a running mistake rather than a navigation error.

Leaving number five, high in a valley, I had followed the curving dip in the contours all the way to the road, turned left and after a hundred metres turned in again to the clearing where one of two large trees was the control feature.

As I went in I realised that a straight line route following the west side of the valley would have been better and faster.

Right from the uphill start, and they are never easy, I had been feeling great and I still was.

At number eight, I waved to Dezso and he raised his hand in reply. Then I turned and was off, racing through the nettles to a small crag about three hundred metres away.

I veered right going up the slope to avoid a small but deepish valley and then followed the line of its far edge, but maybe thirty metres further over, heading slightly down the spur.

Then I could see a ledge of rock sticking up ahead. "That could be it.", I thought. I hit it on top. It was the crag. I went in from the right – a left approach would have been quicker.

I was off again – the slope was really steep now - bouncing along through low, but thick undergrowth, steering round fallen trees and other debris until I hit the path just before it met the forest road deep in the valley.

Then I was flying along the river edge. I spiked the last control, crossed the temporary bridge over the river and raced into the finish.

"Number one," says the announcer, Budapest based Arpad Koscik, before interviewing me in faultless English.

Great forest, I tell him, and top class orienteering. I had made very few mistakes.

I could not be sure how many out there in the arena would understand. By far the majority were Hungarian.

Now all I had to do was wait and see what Gyorgy, the last man out, could do.

He had messed up number three – a tight little re-entrant in amongst many more which I had hit spot on - losing almost ten minutes.

I won in 23m38s; Dezso was runner up in 27m28s.

The Hungarian Cup organisers have a very nice habit taken from the Tour de France cycle race. Each evening, they hold a prize ceremony where the on the day winner in every class is presented with a yellow jersey.

That night I went along to collect mine and celebrate with a free beer, courtesy of the organisers.

I have had a long career in running but I am not used to this – winning.

Despite my successes in the North of England and Scottish championships this year, winning is not and has never been my custom. I should admit that that is not a matter of choice. I am no shrinking violet who shuns such glory nor have I selflessly held back to let others take the glittering prizes. No, in all honesty, I am more accustomed to finishing well down if not propping up the field.

However, in my many years of mixing with winners and talking to them as a journalist I have learned something of the form expected on such occasions.

I have met all types; those who show blatant jubilation to those who either fail to turn up for the prize giving or who almost ashamedly take off the medal when they get off the podium. It is almost as if only Olympic gold is good enough for them.

In occasional defeat, practised winners show either disgust or a "well that's life" stoicism.

The mark of social acceptability in a winner is to show substantial pleasure while never stooping to unmitigated glee.

That's what I opted for as I accepted my yellow jersey and slipped it on.

Whether that is the way I felt inside is another matter. Did I really feel I belonged amongst the exalted? Maybe not.

21

Maybe that's why Day 2 started badly even before I got running. I had the wrong attitude. I faced a longer course with longer legs between some of the controls and I was running in a different part of the forest. I needed to go out there feeling positive, ready for anything. I thought I was but maybe underneath there was a little, worrying sore of doubt.

It was hot again – the late morning temperature reading was twenty-seven degrees on the digital thermometer at the start. That was in the forest. Outside it must have been already into the mid-thirty range.

With one minute to go I picked up a map. Having seen my first day map begin to lose detail just with the sweat from my hands, I decided to take one of the supplied plastic bags to keep this one safe and dry. After all, I would be out there longer. The bag just would not open. The static charge on the plastic was to blame, I suppose, and as the start buzzer went I was still struggling to get it open and slip the map inside.

I set off without having the time to look it over.

I told myself to keep calm and I really thought I'd done just that but I was about to head off in the wrong direction from the start marker – in the wrong direction by all of 180 degrees.

Then I loused up number one. I must have run past the control site, a fallen tree, looking the wrong way. Trouble is the first fallen tree I did see was hidden on the map by the red ink of the control circle. That combined with still trying to come to terms with new mapping and new control descriptions threw my confidence and concentration completely. I was really confused. I must have been looking every way but the right one as I ran by it.

Fallen trees were marked on the map with green T symbols. I had never seen this before. The bigger the tree the longer was the "T".

As I relocated for the third time, I was getting to grips with this and picking them out. This time I got it.

I settled down for number two and hit it faultlessly but in all probability, and that's a very distinct probability, I set off too quickly in search of the next. A longer leg led to a neatly hidden saddle between a ridge and a knoll. Both were well hidden in undergrowth.

Both had lots of green mapping showing thick vegetation around the whole area. That's a sure sign I should have been putting a bit more thought into it.

Half way there I space-time warped – my mind jumped from where I was to a spot very much closer to the control - and started looking for the location and the kite far too early.

As usual, and like everybody else who commits this basic error, I made my surroundings fit the map. The path I crossed became the one next to the control in my mind but it wasn't. The control was not there just around the corner where I expected it to be. Worse still, there was no corner.

I tried this, I tried that, all perfectly respectable attempts to relocate and progress, but the minutes were ticking away.

It was time to remember the next big lesson for life that orienteering has to offer. It is not enough to say I am wrong, I have made a mistake. If you are in deep trouble, the rule is go back. Don't aggravate a mistake by carrying on with the same faulted plan.

That does not mean in orienteering terms that you have to go all the way back and start over or even all the way back to the last control. Just go back as far as necessary, far enough to say with certainty, "I know for sure where I am, what I am at and where I am going."

So…finally I decided to go back, retrace space and time as it were, go through the space-time warp in the opposite direction. That, of course is impossible. I can go back through space but not through time. The time lost – sixteen minutes or so, is lost for ever.

So back I went until I saw the same valley I had crossed just after leaving number two and hit the patch of stony ground I had crossed first time out. I find it on the map, line up my compass and try again. I hit the path again. A flash of light. Awakening. Realisation.

It is this path – I thumb it on the map - not that one. How stupid can I be?

I lined up the compass again and carried on.

"Surely I must be there. No. Carry on still further."

Suddenly everything began to fit. There is the spur partly hidden there in the trees. There is that little valley on the right and there is the saddle.

I run forward.

There is the control marker. Got it. Spiked.

On I went, but try as I might I couldn't get back down to earth. My mind was up a level of excitement cavorting around some six feet above my head and I couldn't rein it in and get it down in my skull again. One small mistake followed another over the controls that followed. Nothing very big and nothing catastrophic, but I had to tell myself, "This is not a good run."

I finished fifth on the day and down in fourth overall

"It was just too green out there," I told Arpad, "but I'll be back tomorrow."

By the look on his face he didn't believe me. He thought I'd blown my chances and that all thought of a comeback was no more than a fantasmagorical dream.

Gyorgy picked up the yellow jersey that night and to be honest looked set for an overall win at the end of the week. His time of around forty-seven minutes was twenty minutes better than mine and put him six minutes up on the best of the others, Dezso, and ten minutes up on me.

Friday came.

Day 3, another hot one, was one for another short run.

I set off across an almost non-existent hill which boasted just enough of a slope to make unwelcome demands on the heart and lungs as I was sucked in by the herd into going a mite too fast.

The first control was a small pit and in that flat, featureless terrain it could have proved really difficult to find but there were so many attack points around, path bends, clearings, thickets and the like that I decided the start marker was as good as any and ran on a rough compass bearing.

I missed it. I might say, I missed it of course, spoiling my chance of a perfect run right at the beginning yet again. This was becoming a habit, a bad habit.

I was dragged off line by another control site but I hit the stopper path at the other side close to a concrete post which seemed to mark the top of the hill. Then with a more careful bearing from there, going in more slowly I hit it spot on.

Of course if I had done that from the start I would have saved time but I had gambled and there had always been the chance that I would have gained a few seconds with an early find.

The second was on the edge of a steep slope which somewhat to my surprise did not go up but dropped away towards some really intricate forest below.

I say to my surprise because the picture in my mind had been completely wrong.

One of the techniques in orienteering is to use the map to build a picture of the control site in your mind. Visualisation, it is called. That's all very well and very useful, if you draw a picture that fits the facts but it can prove disastrous if you build a wrong picture in your head and arrive expecting to find something that exists only in the deep recesses of your brain. It can be difficult to winkle it out and change it to suit reality.

This time it did not matter. A couple of fallen trees lay at the mouth of the re-entrant and I ran quickly past them and slid some fifteen metres down the slope to the marker.

The next looked a humdinger. A tree stump maybe another thirty metres down and two hundred and fifty metres along the slope, but there were an awful lot of turning and weaving contours lying between me and it. There was just one valley after another. The slope ducked in and out with maybe six spurs and valleys on the way, one of them really big.

I opted to give them a miss and take the long way round, climbed part way up the slope and round the head of the big valley to hit a path on the other side. It would give safe fast running.

A girl, looking lost and staring at her map, shouted to me in Hungarian. She obviously wanted help.

This as you might imagine is against the rules but it happens all the time and most people have benefited from it at some time or other, myself included. Usually it has been a club mate I have met up with or, if a stranger, some other lost soul. Always it has been when I have been lost so long that I am out of the running as far as a reasonable position is concerned.

Most people too will stop if it is a child who is lost. This girl was no child. I waved to her and ran on.

After another hot day (35 degrees) and a sweltering run at the Hungarian Cup Five Day Event (Charles Woodward)

This was fast running terrain now and I was doing just that.

At the junction I turned left down the hill and surprise, surprise, there was Dezso coming up. He had started just ahead of me again.

I ran past with a wave and already I could see the stump below me.

Seeing Dezso working, and working hard, going up the slope had made me think.

I had planned to follow that route back up to the path to the next control, a good sized re-entrant on the far side of another big valley just under six hundred metres away.

The path I'd used earlier at the top of the slope went right by it, well maybe missing it by a hundred metres, but it was a big climb back up there and it involved a big semicircular sweep and a lot of extra distance.

I opted to miss out the sweep and make the climb easier at the same time by cutting at an angle across the terrain to meet the path further along. The far bend in the path would be my attack point.

It worked. I kept my run going over the climb, met the path approximately where I intended and veered off it again at the bend and headed towards the head of the valley to avoid the steeper approach and give a straight run into the control site.

Then, there was that girl again. She was still looking lost as she ran towards me. She must have taken my wave as some sort of encouragement.

She fell.

Momentarily I hesitated in my stride, but unable to shout a questioning Hungarian, "OK?" I ran on. She looked all right.

Falls are all part of the orienteering game. You expect fallers to get up relatively uninjured so there is not any real expectation of any real damage.

That is no reason why I should run on by.

Competition in sport, or for that matter at work, in business, you name it, can bring out the nastiness and selfishness in us all.

Running in a German forest on our tour, I fell into a ditch giving my head a really severe dunt. I didn't quite knock myself out but I was dazed and I came to hanging almost upside down from some branches bridging the channel and completely unable to get up.

"Help," I shouted as I struggled to pull myself upright.

A Frenchman, judging by his accent, came by. I recognised him as one of the others on my course.

"Help," I croaked again, my limited French deserting me.

He paused briefly, said something in a questioning tone and then, just as I was expecting a rescuing hand to be offered, he ran off.

Possibly he misconstrued my cries for help as pleasantries telling him that despite all appearances to the contrary, all was well, that I enjoyed lying upside down in a ditch. Maybe he thought I was urging him to run on.

After righting myself and going in pursuit, I beat him into the next control. Needless to say that gave me immense pleasure.

Maybe a nagging conscience had caused him to lose concentration.

My conscience niggled me that day in Hungary. I looked back. The girl was back on her feet. She was still looking sorry for herself but was none-the-worse for wear.

Falling, as I say, is one of the risks of the game. Surprisingly, there are very few really serious injuries.

Such as there are can bring out the best in those around and orienteering can boast some remarkable tales of selfless competitors coming to the aid of others in distress.

One British internationalist came across another runner who had been seriously spiked by a fallen branch. She was already being looked after by another competitor.

She recognised this second woman as the Swiss world number one Simone Luder who had jeopardised her own result to stop and take care of the girl lying bleeding profusely on the forest floor. Someone else had already gone for help.

Without hesitation, the British girl stopped and told Luder to carry on, saying that she would take over and use the already sodden shirt to staunch the flow of blood. She had, she pointed out, less to lose.

She did just that allowing the Swiss to run on to victory, as I recall.

At the Relay World Championship in Hungary, that other multi title winner, Thierry Gueorgiou from France, stopped while on his way to almost certain victory on the anchor leg when he came across a Swedish competitor suffering a similar branch stabbing injury and stayed with him until help came.

Canoeing has a rule which says a competitor must stop to help another in distress.

The unfortunate Hungarian girl, up and running again, was soon behind me and out of mind.

I could see the control standing waiting for me as I turned the head of the valley and headed down the slope.

It was just as I imagined it.

Sometimes you hit it off with a mapper and sometimes you don't.

While there are times the control site is just not the way I thought it would be, a valley at the "wrong" angle, a terrain shape that is just not as I see it, here in Hungary the mapper and I were, if not as one, then at least as nought point nine, nine, nine.

Heading for the penultimate control, another re-entrant but much smaller this time, another tangential run took me to a broken path on top of the spur.

The path broke up just where I needed it most and I left its line a fraction too early. After a moment's hesitation, a quick turn to the right took me to the control.

A steep valley, less than easy to negotiate, slippery with many small drops, lay between me and the finish. A closer look at the map and I would have seen that going out of the re-entrant in the "wrong" direction would have been the right direction. Turning right instead of taking the direct route to the left, would have taken me onto a path that gave both an easy descent and a climb out the other side. Later the splits showed that after losing anything up to an unbelievable minute going into number five, I'd lost another thirty-seconds or more by taking the wrong route out of it. Runs can be won or lost with less.

No bother, I spiked the last control and sprinted downhill for the finish.

Dezso came down the track maybe half a minute later.

I washed off the dust and salt in the stream and drank some much needed water.

Strangely enough, for all the high temperatures which had others complaining day on day, I was not suffering from the heat while running in the forest.

I remember reading that as you get older you produce more salt in your sweat. That means that drop for drop, the sweat uses up more heat as it evaporates. Normally, by that I mean back home, this means that the sweat does not evaporate so easily so oldies can finish a run with faces streaming and vests soaked.

In the high Hungarian temperatures, where we were enjoying a dry heat, there was no such problem and I was benefiting, the sweat was exerting its full cooling effect and I was taking the heat in my running stride, so to speak.

We were over a kilometre from assembly but a radio or wire link from the finish kept those waiting up to date with results.

As I walked and jogged down the forest road, Arpad was already announcing my win and that I had moved back into the lead.

It was touching that he had time for everyone. So often, announcers concentrate, quite rightly, on the elite competitors running the longest and most physically demanding courses. That's life.

Arpad, on the other hand, opened it up making it more of a day for all concerned covering all the age group competitions and the nationalities taking part.

So - another win and another yellow jersey. Gyorgy had suffered a disaster taking seven minutes to find the tree stump at number three and twelve to find the little valley second from last. He was back in third overall but, and it was a big "but", that I overlooked in the euphoria of my win, he was only 1m 17s down on me with Dezso in second less than a minute down.

I was beginning to enjoy these middle distance events. Two wins out of two.

I have always maintained that real orienteering is the classic.

At the World Championships, the men's classic was usually won in just under ninety minutes.

That seemed to be a fairly crucial time.

Ninety minutes takes the average top runner into "hitting the wall" country. Hitting the wall in orienteering is not quite the same as in marathon running. It is not a physical loss of control with the legs turning to putty beneath you. That can come later.

It is the brain that suffers first in orienteering. After about ninety minutes it can go into a gooey sort of limbo affecting both the legs and the mind. The more mistakes a runner makes early on and the more time lost, the more likely they are to get into "bonking" territory but then if they run too slowly to avoid early mistakes....... Well, it is a tantalising matter of finding the right balance.

"What about the women?" you are asking. Well, of course it applies to them too, but whereas women run the same marathon distance as men, in orienteering they have not quite obtained par status. Their classic runs used to be geared to a sub-eighty minute winning time, so while finishers down the field could well find themselves suffering in ninety minute territory, it played no part in deciding the top placings.

That was all many years ago now and of no more than of historical significance for those coming up through the sport now.

For them, orienteering is a multi-distance sport where increasingly the accent is on shorter distance running.

Yet, no one is flying across the continent to take part in a five day sprint series.

So, being a bit of an old timer in the sport, I have been reticent in accepting the new formats.

Urban running is out of the question with my dodgy achilles likely to give trouble if I do venture too much onto the roads, but as for the others, I have had money and time in mind rather than a "it didn't happen in my young day" attitude. I like course length value and a longer time in the forest for my money.

I must say I enjoyed these middle distance, or to be more exact forest sprint, outings in Hungary. In quality terrain, they allowed "fast" running, over a distance and time that kept tiredness out of the equation.

To be fair I must admit that my mistakes, the big mistakes and really big mistakes, have not generally come when I am tired.

Many come as I hit the initial low in oxygen supply.

Noticeably when I have had a couple of layoffs due to injury and my fitness has fallen away, I would find that in my first few events back I would make mistakes round about the third control or fifteen minutes into the run. I would prime myself to take care as I approached that point.

Then after maybe a couple of months more of training it would be the sixth control that signalled danger.

Running fit, it is the hour mark that signals a loss of concentration and danger.

Many of my mistakes, as was evident on Day 2 in Hungary, come in the first few controls when possibly I am running too confidently and taking insufficient care.

I went out on Day 4's long run primed to take care. I told myself, "Go for a perfect run. Use basic technique. Remember CASH."

The first control, a knoll over a spur and up a shallow valley from the start was not where I thought it would be. It seemed to be further round to the right than I had anticipated. Looking now at the map I can see that the bottom contour of the spur is not only less curved, the curve is further to the "East", so I can see why I had read them wrongly.

I hit the control with no trouble and while the discrepancy niggled it was quickly forgotten.

Heading for two, a tiny crag amongst a series of pits, my plan was to head up the valley and follow a line of thick vegetation and attack from its south east corner. At the same time I did not want to get too far in to the thicker going for it would slow me down. Being in two minds is never a good idea.

Ever so subtly the valley swung to the South east and following this new imperceptible change in line took me wide of the big thicket. I could see it off to the right but I could also see that the young birch around my legs were indeed much thicker over there and I thought I could avoid their hindrance and judge my approach from a distance.

I crossed the forest road. There was the thicket away of over to the right.

There should have been a shallow re-entrant on my left but I could not see it.

Getting worried I carried on. Getting more worried I began to waver and trot aimlessly. By now, a crag, any crag should have been standing out like a Saturn rocket.

I could have run for the area of fight and come in again but now it all seemed a bit unclear from where I was standing and not the inviting option I once thought it to be.

I struck a small thicket but could not place it on the map. I started to wander on again only to be surprised at seeing a big depression ahead – a really big depression. I was close to panic. The only big depression around was over a hundred metres past the control.

It was time not just to find the control but to take control, mental control. I turned around and headed for the distant area of thicket ready to make a fresh start but did so on a compass bearing based on the big depression on the map.

Then not so much by chance as on a calculated risk, I found a biggish hole. I paused. Further over there was another.

I was in the right area. These were obviously part of the patch of small depressions. My control, my crag, was either marginally to the North or to the South of where I stood. I opted to go north. And....there it was, another hole in the ground with a rocky rim on one side. That was my tiny crag. You could fall off this one with no danger. Finding it was the problem. It had cost me the best part of four minutes.

You have no idea how the tension slips away at times like that.

Finding a control, running over a summit say and seeing it lying there where you expected it to be, is, as I have said, a bit like sinking a putt in golf. It is one of the major satisfactions of the game. It gives you a little surge of pleasure a momentary high.

On the other hand, running over a summit full of expectation only to find that there is no control gives a terrible, sinking feeling.

One of my faults in the sport is slowing, sometimes even stopping, before going into a control. I think I have a dread of the control not being there and the disappointment that comes with finding just that.

So finding number two sent my spirits soaring and after that things went well.

161

Number three was the little thicket I had met up with during my wandering. It was easy. I'd been there already.

Then it was across the road back onto the slope near the start and into an intricate little loop of three crags before heading back up the slope to number seven.

A long road run (I say long but I mean long in orienteering leg terms - it was no more that seven hundred and fifty metres) - took me to number eight, another crag a hundred or so metres into the woods. Then I was off again across a fairly featureless headland with more tracks on the ground than on the map heading for into a steepish valley for number nine. Another steep valley crossing ended on another broad shoulder where the crag I was looking for was pinpointed by a fallen tree neatly lined up both on the ground and on the map.

After that I was heading for home, plunging down into the valley through a maze of fallen timber, leaping the branches, riding the slithers when others slid from under my feet, and then I was sprinting down the path to the finish. It might have looked if I was dicing with danger and surely due a fall but I was on a runner's high. I just didn't care.

Not bad, I thought, as I spiked the finish. Dezso was there already and that was a bit disappointing, but then maybe he had started much earlier than me. I hadn't checked but no, it wasn't bad. The splits were to show that I had four first places and two-seconds. I thought I might have won again.

Back in the assembly things were not too clear. I had had an earlier start that day and there was just a danger that one of the later starters could better my time.

One of them did. Control number two not only cost me four minutes, it turned out to have cost me day victory as well.

Gyorgy Varga had a superb run which saw him top the leader board from control four onwards.

I finished runner up but all of three minutes down with my time of 39m4s and in second place overall.

On Saturday evening we took the Woodwards back to our hotel for the Erzsebet baked ham "special" and it really was a bit of a country style delicacy. It went down very well with a couple of beers.

As we sat there in the garden the first drops of rain fell and we were forced to move first under the canopy and then indoors as it started in earnest.

As well as paying for the meal that evening we decided to settle the bill for the week. It was higher than expected. This was partly due, I think, to the florint losing ground against the euro and our landlords had always insisted it was a euro rate we were paying. I was in no position to argue the point. They had a print out of a highly detailed account for us to peruse. Imagine our shock when we found we had been charged extra for the coffee option on the breakfast menu! Our Hungarian guide book had warned that it was always as well to check a bill for it is not uncommon for little extras to be added in restaurants. This was not the first time we had come across it. In one café we were charged for the milk. The landlady, as I have said, did not speak English but she knew we were far from amused when we laughed in disbelief. When she came back, countering with the suggestion that maybe we should pay for the air conditioning as well we decided she had won and to call it a day.

So the weather had broken as promised and steady rain saw us finish the night in the bar at the Woodwards' hotel where a string of folks, who had come from far and near for an open air arena pop concert in a nearby quarry, had dropped in for "refreshments". Good luck to them we thought. Outside it was cold, wet and miserable.

Looking forward to the next day, Charlie asked me how I would run it.

It was going to be a chasing start – still staggered but with the time intervals set by the times over the first four days. This makes a big difference. Normally when you cross the finish line, you maybe know that you have had a dandy run, you maybe know too, if the commentary has picked you up, that you are leading the field, and if there is no-one still to come who could beat you, that you have won. In chasing start orienteering, first across the line wins. It turns the sport from a time trial into a race.

Gyorgy's total time was 1m40s better than mine so I would set off 1m40s behind him in the final.

Charlie's question made me think about something I was maybe trying to ignore.

"Catch him up fast, hang on and go all out to beat him on the run in," I joked.

I knew that an all out aggressive approach could spell disaster. If I didn't blow up early in the chase and lose the running in my legs, not enough care at one control could see me racing around like the proverbial headless chicken. Not only would I leave him to romp home untested but there was every chance those starting after me might pull me in, go by and knock me out of the medal placings.

"No," I joked again but joked seriously. "I'll forget him. I'm going all out for that perfect run."

The perfect run might still elude me but chasing it rather that Gyorgy was the right thing to do.

22

So come Sunday, there I was standing nervously in a rain soaked forest looking forward to a run which could give me my best ever result.

Thierry Gueorgiou says of such moments, "Being relaxed is the key. You have to do everything as if D-day were just an ordinary day in your life."

He reminds, "It is important to see that even if you spoil the race it is not the worst thing that can happen in your life."

That is sound logic. For my part, I was concentrating in going for that perfect run, but I still had to slip off for yet another toilet squat in the forest.

We had set out early with the car thermometer reading thirteen degrees – shades of home. What a change!

I have an early start just after ten – 10:06.40 to be precise - so after parking, I gear up quickly, say my goodbyes, welcome everyone's good wishes and start out on the long jog to the start area.

Before leaving I checked the run in. Just as well too for it has been changed from the first day. I can't see the last control but I leave with the layout in my head. I know what to expect. I will know what lies ahead if it does come down to a head to head racing finish.

At the start I am first to arrive, but again that gives me time to warm up, check the layout, collect and check my control description list and find the race "bib" which gives my age class and position.

The start clock tells me the temperature has climbed to fifteen but it is raining lightly, or is it? Maybe it is just the drips from the trees.

Tents have been put up against the weather. We go into the first box six minutes before take off to allow time for the officials to check and sort us into order.

I can see the start kite about thirty metres ahead and while the woods around us are quite dense, they open out the other side of the start. A hill rises just ahead and there is a line of young trees and bushes heading straight up it, one of those rides which has filled in over the years. It will be on the map.

Ten minutes have passed and the early starters are all here. There aren't many of us. The courses have been well staggered to avoid overcrowding here and at the finish.

I look around unobtrusively, like a B-movie spy, for my rival. I have not managed to pick him out in the crowds at the start on other days. However, the number one bib is missing from the rack so he has to be here somewhere.

Maybe he is that big fella over there. He's wearing a raincoat which covers any number he might be wearing.

Crikey, he looks strong. Come the start he'll whip that raincoat off and go galloping off through the forest. He'll eat me up on the hills. We're running around 3k but there's 110m of climb out there to contend with.

I shouldn't let it get to me but there's much propaganda for we little guys to contend with. Think how often you hear commentators say something like, "He's not very big but....." The "but" could be any number of things that excuse this wee man's audacity for just being there taking on the big men who are seen as natural winners.

I interviewed one of Britain's top swimmers once. She was national record holder over 100m and was close to taking top international honours.

However, she reported, the sports scientists drafted into the sport had told her she was too small to succeed.

Bad science and poor use of statistics had led them to deal the woman a crucial blow to her morale and confidence. She gave up swimming shortly afterwards.

Unlike racism, sexism, and ageism, sizeism is the great, unrecognised discrimination in society.

Small guys have to take much ribbing that passes for fun in our society but they never quite get used to it.

Of course some big fellas have the same problem. People will pick on anyone they can if they get away with it.

166

I heard one girl say recently that she always envied smaller women in orienteering.

She stood at maybe five foot nine or ten inches.

"I always think how much less weight they have to carry up the hills," she explained.

It all comes down to power to weight ratio I am told.

So standing there something deep inside nags at me about negative thinking and that this is no way for a potential winner to behave. After all I've beaten Gyorgy two days out of four and if it had not been for my disaster on Day 2 I might have been heading the field today with a substantial lead. I say might because no doubt he could say the same thing about one of his bad runs. It is still a relief to pick out this other guy with the number one bib standing over the other side of the waiting area. He is much more my size.

After a few moments he comes over and offers his hand. We shake and wish each other good luck in our different languages. At least I think that's what he said. It's that kind of moment when smiles mean more than words.

Then a few minutes more and it is time to go.

I watch as he sets off past the start kite and veers to the left.

The minutes are ticking way. The starter has his hand on my chest holding me in. I can see the seconds ticking away on the clock. 10:06 and then the seconds - 35, 36, 37, 38, 39, 40. The restraining hand drops away and I am off.

Pull the map off its nail, check it is the right one, take in the shape of the course..... an S shaped curve.

First control, a re-entrant is almost five hundred metres away. How to get there? Play it safe. Follow the defunct overgrown ride over the first hill, turn left down the path into the valley and then right up the next valley. The marker is high on the far slope.

No time wasted. I'm already on the move while I take this in and make the decision.

This is a stiff climb so early in the course, before I get my second wind. I'm breathing hard but keeping a steady jog going.

The vegetation is on the thick side. I toy with the idea of slipping down to the right in more open forest but not for long. That is the wrong side. Stick to the plan unless a change is to my obvious advantage.

167

I seem to have been climbing a long, long time. I stall. No, keep on going. I should pass to the right of the summit.

The waist high vegetation in the ride is getting thicker. Ease over to the left and head for the summit. Don't lose the overall direction.

Then there I am going down into the valley beyond. I can see the second valley over to the right. I strike across country and aim for the steep east facing slope.

My eye follows the line of crags at the top and from where I am up on the opposite wall I can see the control. My heart skips a beat, a metaphorical beat, nothing to do with needing a beta blocking booster.

Check the map. Yes, that's it. Head for it.

The marker disappears behind the shoulder as I head up the slope but I follow the line and hit it spot on. Check control number and spike

So now it is turn to the left and head for number two.

It is another re-entrant about another five hundred metres away but the straight line route runs down sharply into another gully, up the other side and across the edge of a hill before another descent into the big valley beyond where the feature is nestling at the base of the far slope.

One approach would be to skirt round the base of the plateau and run up the valley but I opt for a reasonably straight line run on a rough compass bearing using a patch of thicker wood as a check.

My legs are feeling good now and despite some rough underfoot going with stones and fallen branch debris the running is fairly easy even if it is meandering.

I hit the top of the slope, locate on a little valley to my left, and head down at an angle ready to check off a couple of fallen trees on the way.

I look ahead, and can pick out the opposite slope and almost immediately my route choice pays off for again I can see the marker long before I reach it. Again using the high approach has paid dividends. If I had been running up the valley, I would not have seen it until I was right on top of the feature.

The planner could have made this leg more difficult by choosing a feature on the descent slope, one of the fallen trees maybe.

In I go, spike and come out on a one hundred and fifty metre leg running south.

Until now everything has been going fine. Could this be the day for the perfect run? I don't even think about it. There are seven more controls. I concentrate on concentration.

I am heading for the slope just ahead and a small crag.

I see the slope but I don't see the crag, and what is that massive boulder doing there down to the left?

I check the map. There it is. I have run too far. Forgot to pace count and I didn't notice that I should have dropped a contour.

I look back and see the crag about twenty metres back.

No problem but thirty-seconds or so wasted and good bye again to that perfect run.

The route to number four takes me past the big boulder. I hit the path beyond and recognise a woodland education display board. I think it is one we passed on the way to the start the previous day.

Little things mean a lot is the old saying and that is certainly true in orienteering. That little dip in concentration is enough to throw me and I veer off to the right.

I cross a couple of paths and hit the spur beyond before cooling it down and thinking where I am going. The spur is what I'm looking for, but I'm looking for a tree stump on the nose over a hundred metres away.

I hit the rocky knoll at the end and there is a marker down in a little gully. Stupidly I dive down to check it, forgetting completely about what I am looking for. That's more time wasted.

Out again, I race round the promontory, and there is it, my marker and the stump.

I turn to leave heading down the slope and there he is. I'm sure it's him. Gyorgy. I've caught him. In fact I've passed him.

It turns out that he had been opening up time and distance on me. He had been going fast, maybe too fast. At number four everything had gone haywire. He had spent over six minutes searching for the marker further down the slope while, despite my mistakes I had taken more than three minutes out of him.

Right, now forget him. There's a job to do. Make the rest of the run as near perfect as possible.

Next in line is a big, shallow depression to the North.

I take a very rough compass line aiming to use the path running from the junction below as my attack feature.

I hit the big path and there is a junction.

I head out across the flat. This is marvellous running. I'm enjoying it.

I have forgotten to do the double check with my compass that the moment required. Is the path running in the right direction? Am I running in the right direction? Suddenly, the ground is starting to rise. That should not be

"Stop", I tell myself but I've got to say it a few times more before I listen.

I look round. Gyorgy has been following me and is about forty metres back.

The temptation is to run to the right and hope everything will fall into place. With my day two debacle in mind I tell myself and force myself to go back. I pass Gyorgy who is standing bemused. He already knows he has committed the cardinal orienteering blunder - following the idiot up ahead.

I get back to the path junction. There's the path I should have used. I take a quick compass check and head off again.

Looking ahead I can see Gyorgy still searching around. Then as I look a woman runs into a dip and then comes out again. That's it. Orienteering can be full of such flukes. I'm on line. Good.

However, there is Gyorgy, he has seen her too and he is in to number five and out again just as I approach. Again, he is in front..... by seconds.

A path leads most of the way to number six – another tree stump - but it is a vague path in places and having Gyorgy ahead is helpful.

I head off at an angle up the slope before he does and while I still go into the control just as he is leaving I claim back a couple of seconds.

Now it is time to keep an eye on him as well as the map. This is what "Chasing Start" orienteering is all about. It is matter of using your opponents as well as the map and if necessary fight it out in a head to head sprint down the finish funnel. If it comes to that, can I beat him?

Right now I'm looking for a small crag, slightly hidden by the vegetation if the map is anything to go by. It is on the far slope of next shallow valley.

A big patch of thick forest and then a smaller one, both to the left, are there to pick off then it is down into the valley.

There's Gyorgy. Crikey he's running fast. If it comes to that sprint down for the line, he could beat me.

There must be something slightly absurd about two of life's ancient has-beens melting it hell for leather through the woods like this but, man, it's great fun.

However, Gyorgy is off line. He is away over near that little clearing, the one that gives me a line into the control.

I run straight, sure my line is the best and there it is. The vegetation isn't as thick as I feared it might be.

As I run up the slope, I see Gyorgy has changed direction and is coming in from the right.

He is pushing it. He is racing. Again he beats me to the control and he has opened the gap.

A hundred metre wide barrier of young birches running along a ridge stand between us and the next control. A big detour would take you round it but that would also mean cutting backwards and much extra running. It would be more than twice the distance.

We both decide on the straight forward approach cutting through the thick trees to the other side.

We both hit an island of open trees in the middle but while he heads right I opt for the narrower neck in the thicket and turn to my left over a slight summit.

I get out the other side and, while I know where I should be, it is worth checking.

There is a boulder just ahead. I look at the map. There it is. The control is a boulder along the thicket edge to my right. I turn. Gyorgy is about thirty metres away looking lost. He shouts something but as I run towards him he picks up the cue, turns and heads along the line of the thicket.

He spikes it first then I do too but he is still that elusive few seconds ahead.

Then it is down the slope towards number nine – the last control. This is not an easy one. The slope's curving so both keeping on line and knowing exactly where you are at the same time are difficult.

Nine is another quarry shaped re-entrant just off the major trail that runs down to the finish arena.

Gyorgy hits the path. Possibly I've pulled him in a fraction. He turns to his right as I approach from behind.

Momentarily I am about to follow. Then I stop. I look at the map. The control site is backed by a thicket, just after a junction with a smaller path.

I look to the right. Gyorgy is approaching a thicket OK, but.....something tells me he has got it wrong.

I look the other way, down the path. The finish is down there too. There is a bigger thicket and I see too what could be the re-entrant.

I start to run.

There's the path junction.

Then I'm into the re-entrant. I spike and I'm out again.

No time now for thinking. No time for looking behind. I'm running and it feels good, feels really good.

I hit the arena. This is the perfect run in....the perfect shape for flying..... downhill then into an S shape, swinging round the big tree to the right and then round through the other trees to the left and on to the finish line.

Music is playing, the man on the mic says I'm coming in to win. The people are shouting – they are not shouting for me - I'm not on my own on the run in. Who knows who they are shouting for? Who cares? It just feels oh so good, so alive.

A final moment of confusion with the finish markers which are placed a bit past the banner, and then I'm there. Done. Finished. Number One.

Seventeen-seconds later Gyorgy finishes. He shakes my hand. I pat his back. I know how he must feel. To be beaten is one thing. To be beaten because you have "cocked it up" at the last control is "the pits".

After a while I migrate back to the finish funnel and join in the applause for the stream of runners still crossing the line. It will take a couple of more hours at least for everyone to finish.

The other early starters are still coming in. Many of them wear day bibs like my own showing they are chasing top places and medals in their age groups. Others do not.

For all and sundry, racing down into the arena, past the cheering people brings a light to their faces and a spring to their steps.

172

None of them are highly trained professional athletes.

The spindly ten year old girl bouncing along as if gravity not only does not matter but does not exist and the muscled twenty-one year old powering home, kicking up dust, are "flying", momentarily exalted, momentarily out of themselves.

Both are on a drug free high.

I clap and clap again, shout them all on repeatedly.

If the crowd and the cheers and joy of running can light up faces in this way, who needs pills?

23

That afternoon, the medal ceremony under a line of national flags over, we drove the Woodwards to Lake Balaton to start the next stage of their holiday and then packed our bags ready for an early departure next morning to take the car back to Bratislava.

We were off to Vienna for three days of music, galleries, empire architecture, city streets, city restaurants and city cafés.

The train ride produced another first.

As we drew into the Sudbahnhoff platform in the Austrian capital four twenty-or-so year olds ambled down the corridor towards the door.

The first paused.

"Can I help you with your case?" he asked.

"Do I really look like I need help?" was my first thought. Is that what I have come to? Is that what life has become – am I a little old man who needs help to get his case off the train?

Now my case has a history. It was a Slovakian case bought in Bratislava last time around after my then case fell apart in the streets of Komarno.

A wheel jammed and I didn't notice. It was overheated by the friction as I pulled the case along the pavements and melted its bearing.

The new case we bought cost almost twice as much in Slovakia than in the same high street supermarket at home.

That wasn't its only fault. It had only one handle – at the end. Without a side handle it was more difficult to lift.

So, if my first response to the young man was less than welcoming, it did not last long.

I quickly assessed the situation, swallowed my pride, broke into a smile and said, "Yes, please."

As he was about to lift it he was lightly pushed aside by his massive six foot square companion. He grabbed the handle and swung the case off the floor with absolute ease and a few steps later landed it on the platform. So age does have its advantages.

We arrived back home to an orienteering hiatus. The British sport was still in its summer close down. I had an empty feeling. Something was missing where my orienteering should have been. All the excitement and the social mixing of competition were suddenly gone.

Our next event, the Lakes Five Day was scheduled for mid-August and to make things worse, it looked like there might be a problem in maintaining fitness and training until then.

It was not that I had lost impetus. No. I was injured again.

There is always the danger that overtraining can lead to breakdown.

Muscles, tendons and joints develop small injuries during one run which the next run aggravates and so on, leading to a more major injury which finally cannot be ignored.

My problem was almost certainly linked to a change in running style.

At a conference back in June, a cross-country internationalist passed on some basic technique info. He introduced, what was for me, a new approach in foot control, bringing the foot forward in a horizontal position before placing it– ball first – on the ground. Video investigation backed up his suggestions and an interval session proved it gave me both faster cruising times and longer stride length even if the cadence was slower.

My first day back I took on an hour of rough trail running. By half way a niggle was developing in the ligaments around my ankle. By the end it was a nagging pain that came with every stride and I was hobbling by the time I reached home.

In the next few days I did some gym and weights work and a couple of cycle rides. This cross-training was certainly effective but while it has its place in the overall scheme of training for running, I agree with Martensson, it does not make up for running itself.

The next day I tested the ankle out but the pain was still there so it was back to the bike, this time for five days.

175

There were just eleven days left now before the "Lakes 5" so the pressure was on.

A one hour map run, and a forty minute club outing on the same day got things going. Then I put in a few days of intervals on the flat and the hills.

After another rest day I put in a ninety minute one man training event on one of our local maps.

I was running well but by the time I got back to the car I was in pain again. This time it was my back, in at the spine at the base of the rib cage.

There was no denying that foot position was the root of the problem.   Run the old way and I was OK.   Use the "new technique" and the pain returned.

The next day I rested the foot, and then went walking the next.

Maybe I needed more walking practice.

There was less than a week left and it was beginning to look like I might have to walk my way round the Lakes 5 too.

An easy run with two days to go proved things were on the mend but I arrived in Cumbria with my back feeling tender from the drive and everything still up in the air.

We joined up with our daughter Nicola for this trip.

A former junior internationalist and university blue in the sport she began giving me trouble in our terrain runs in her early twenties but like many others, she drifted out of the sport as work and other interests developed.   In the last few years she has been making a bit of a comeback, so meeting up like this lent an extra dimension to our trip and the competition.

We rented a rudimentary cottage from a hotel in Milnethorpe, an "old" A6 village just a mile or so from the M6 and just out of the Lake District proper. It is close to the coastal villages of Morecombe Bay, however, and provided a pleasant escape from the Lake District holiday crowds.

It also provided easy access to both the motorway and the Barrow road and thus to the widely spread event venues.

Unlike the Hungarian multi day, the Lakes 5 had no pretensions to keeping things local.   It was a tourist holiday event which had everyone travelling widely from the event centre in Coniston to Keswick, Shap and Kendal.

The Lakes 5 comes up every four years, which is just about time for everyone to forget the long uphill walks to the starts and back down after finishing. After four years they remember only the Lake District's reputation for providing the best orienteering in England.

It is a reputation I have never fully understood. Despite boasting widespread and extensive woodland full of complex terrain shapes, so many orienteering events are held on open fell land with big climbs and rough underfoot going.

The event also has a reputation for being dogged by rain, often of torrential proportions.

That might explain why we were taking it on for the first time.

It lived up to its reputation.

It rained, not heavily and not all the time, but most days it was threatening. In some ways that made the sunny spells all the more welcome.

On Day 2 we had a long, wet walk from the car park to the assembly field and it poured during the event.

We benefited from our early starts but it must have been slithery going on some of the churned up, muddy, woodland slopes for those who started later in the day. They were out there while we were sheltering in our tent back at the finish.

Tea and jammy scones in the nearby lakeside hotel went down a bomb afterwards.

The next day, the event at Thirlmere was postponed because the car park field was too wet.

It had taken us an hour's driving to get there and it was not until we were about to turn into the country road at the head of the lake that we found a notice saying to come back on the Wednesday, which had been scheduled as the midweek break.

It was a pity, for once the morning rain cleared we enjoyed a beautiful day with a boat trip down Derwent Water. We got off at the southern end for a climb up the side of the Lodore Falls and picnic at the top before continuing the trip back to Keswick.

Well, the next day heavy showers were again visible to the North as we headed again up the M6. The sky cleared and all seemed set for what promised to be a day of technically demanding navigating on the moors and in some very complex forest.

That reckoning didn't take water authority reasoning into account.

They were concerned that the wet parking field would become a quagmire and mud would escape into the reservoir. They were worried too by their understanding that the next day the farmer would bring his sheep off the fells and hold them in the same field. It was argued that the sheep purls would join the mud soup along with any diseases they might carry and that this more dangerous mixture would escape into the water supply.

The venue was dropped. Five days became four days.

On our way back to our cottage we travelled through the beautiful Grasmere area where poet William "golden daffodils" Wordsworth spent much of his life.

Ignore his liking for trapping woodcock and stealing ravens' eggs and he could well be the orienteers' poet for he had a deep feeling for the great outdoors.

"… (I've) escaped from the vast city, where I long had pined a discontented sojourner…" he says, like urban orienteers from Lisbon to antipodean Auckland, as they roll into the event centre parking.

He's my type of seat of the pants operator too -

"I look about and should the chosen guide
Be nothing better than a wandering cloud
I cannot miss my way."

He should be so lucky. He should be so good. There's orienteering skill!

The Lakes' walks to the starts too lived up to their reputation.

The first day put them into perspective.

Five or more miles of narrow roads had taken us from Shap to the parking field at Bampton, close to Haweswater. It is amazing how quickly after leaving the M6 you are twisting and edging your way through deepest English countryside.

Sitting back in the sun enjoying a coffee and cake – a staple diet when runs bridge lunch time - we could see runners high on the hill opposite. Slowly we realised that the ones we could see were not competing. They had finished and were heading back. They were really far off. It was certainly a long way home. The route to the start was even further with a formidable climb into the bargain.

It was a tough walk, but standing up at the start waiting for the minutes to pass until it was time to go, the almost circular panorama of hills taking in the best of the Lake District plus the Pennine tops to the East was nothing short of breath taking and well worth the thirty minute tramp.

The penultimate day at Caw Hill to the south of Coniston was even more horrendous with a steep, muddy, woodland path descent followed by a climb up the road on the other side of the valley. High on the far slope it went past the finish so it was going to be a long, slithery walk home as well, squeezing past the late starters going out as we did so.

Lakes 5 terrain too was as expected.

Only the second day venue at Guards Wood just outside Coniston had woods of any great size.

Despite the rain I had my best run of the week there.

I say despite the rain, but the full "despite" list is almost endless.

It starts with despite the long, three kilometre walk from the car park.

The rain started on the walk to the start – just half a mile this one.

I get there and join the others sheltering under the trees.

Then as my glasses misted up I notice I have brought the wrong ones – my distance lenses rather than the varifocals.

I run the half mile back to our tent in the assembly area and change them, then hurry back to the start area.

By this time my glasses are thick with rain water so I take them off to clean and dry them. At this point one of the lenses comes loose and falls on the grass. I have lost two pairs of glasses in the past after having them flicked off by branches so I suffer a momentary panic.

Not to worry; this time I find the lens easily enough but then, with the time running down increasingly fast, I struggle to get it back into its frame.

I calm myself, relaxing my shoulders and the muscles all the way down my back, breathing slowly and deeply.

Then it's time to go.

I tear off the black bin liner I am wearing against the rain - it would make for very hot going on the run - and move into the start area. I pick up my control description list and struggle again as I slip it into the wet holder. There – done it. I put it on my wrist and pull the band tight, only to have the thing burst open with the fastener irreparably broken.

I struggle again to mend it as I move up to the front line, and I am still struggling as the beeper goes and it is time to go.

So off I go juggling compass, map and the defunct control description holder and trying to read the map at the same time.

As starts go it has all the makings of a major orienteering disaster.

However, that's not what happens.

I get into competition mode on the way to number one and then everything picks up more or less like clockwork – well probably more "less" than "more".

Down the hill through thick trees and rough going to five I have only a vague picture in mind of the terrain around the stream at the bottom of the hill. I am too slow. Slanting runs down hill always make for difficult navigation. I misread a steep slope for a crag, pick the hill on the left instead of the one on the right and lose a minute more checking it out.

So this is not going to be the perfect run I am after either.

Six – perfect; seven – put in an unnecessary climb instead of a lower level detour; eight – brilliant; nine – good path run followed by a stiff climb and a vague finish but spot on. Then ten – I navigated round the wrong bracken patch and climbed too high up the spur. I found myself just over the fence from the start field which threw me momentarily but made for easy repair.

Minor errors followed too at fifteen, sixteen and seventeen but I was moving well throughout and raced home for a time just over the hour, my personal barrier.

I was fifth fastest on the run in – picking up a forty year old as he went by – and at the end of the day finished tenth overall out of sixty-three starters.

Since I was running up a class I was well pleased with that and I still am.

Most of the runs, as I say, were on fell terrain of varying degrees of tough, rough going. Physically demanding, but on the face of it, posing less of a problem as far as navigation is concerned. You can look well ahead and pick out your landmarks. On the other hand, the wider vistas, seeing more of the terrain, more crags, more hills, can overtax the brain and big spaces with little to see can make for big relocation problems.

That first day at Swindale, near Shap, is a case in point.

It is a fabulous day and so is the running. I leave number three to head out on some really crisp going, short grass over the summits, many sheep tracks to be picked up, very fast.

A minor mistake at the first had again knocked out a perfect run but that was quickly forgotten. It was out of this world, to be running with a map, up there high in the hills with little or no wind and the sun shining.

Leaving number seven I detour off the straight line route to pick up a grass track. These days with shepherds no longer walking the heights, crook in hand, dogs at heel, but cruising along in their four by four buggies, hill terrain is rich in such tracks.

They change a lot and this one is no exception. It just keeps on going and going, well past the point where it stops on the map.

All the time it is heading towards the craggy bluff down in the valley that I have picked as my attack point.

I really am flying. The splits will show that I am fourth fastest over this leg and that I pick up six places to move into twelfth.

This has all the makings of being a fine even if not a perfect run, or so it seems until some ten minutes later, I top a knoll full of expectation only to find control number ten is not nestling at the side of a marsh below.

Back at nine a look at the map tells me that I am looking for a couple of little hills to run in from. Looking down the hill I can see two hills with many people running around them. That's where I'm heading.

("How about checking your compass?" you will be asking, or "What did you say about jumping to conclusions?")

The map tells me there is another track over to the left which could take me right past the control but it is almost two hundred metres away so I may not use it.

As it is I follow an "elephant track" going off to the left through the marsh. The rushes are long here and the marsh looks wet so I follow the "track" through.

As I come out the other side I can still see the people going into controls down to my right and I turn and head in that direction, heading as fast as I can right into the pits of disappointment.

In retrospect, of course, I can see that back at number nine I could not possibly have seen the little hills around control ten. There was a spur over five metres high in the way. That "elephant track" through the marsh was heading in exactly the right direction, over the spur and straight on. (Remember what you said about using my compass, jumping to conclusions?)

There I am checking out likely markers all away off target.

Remembering the lesson from Hungary I consider going back to nine to start the leg again but, where is it? Looking back, the hillside is remarkably lacking in features and any that are there are difficult to identify, especially since I have no idea where I am on the map.

This is a situation where GPS equipment could come in useful allowing the runner to retrace their steps, guided electronically, to the previous control.

Many orienteers use basic GPS which records position and speed details which can be downloaded after they finish but these have no map display.

GPS units with map displays are banned in the sport everywhere except Sweden, and taking a wrist or hand GPS reader is banned at IOF championships.

The Swedes argue that using GPS is slower than using a map and compass but I suspect they have not considered the benefits which lost orienteers might stand to gain.

I look for the track. It isn't there of course. I check out a narrow re-entrant but again I can't locate it on the map.

I head back to the knoll and follow it round still convinced I must be only a little wrong and maybe if I go a bit further I'll find the control, but of course it isn't there.

It is not so hard to say you are wrong. Believing it is another matter.

A woman, cursing her own stupidity, stops by me as I stand there looking down at a very short stretch of wall below this mind blasting knoll, a wall almost hidden by earth and vegetation.

"It's a wall," I tell her. "Where is it on the map?"

"It's here," she says, "these two crags. That one is the wall."

She points on the map and I see for the first time where I am - over two hundred metres south east of where I should be. Not just that, I'm standing with my map round the wrong way.

A leg that should have cost me four minutes at the most ended up at almost sixteen. Without that mistake I would have set up my week with a possible top ten place.

Of course, everyone else could say something the same.

25

I should really feel at home in the Lake District.

Both the Lakes villages and Birnam have hills on their doorstep and both areas have connections with famous children's writer, Beatrix Potter.

The Peter Rabbit author lived in London as a child but her family spent their summer holidays in both the Lake District and the Birnam-Dunkeld area.

While the world knows her best as the writer of twenty-three children's books, Potter also became a notable scientific expert on fungi and lichen following up on a fascination kindled by Perthshire naturalist Charles McIntosh. She produced learned tomes on the subject with highly praised illustrations.

In her forties, she moved to the Lakes to live, marrying a local lawyer, buying a number of farms and became a keen conservationist.

Birnam has a children's garden in memory of Potter and Peter Rabbit in the centre of the village and a notable exhibition in the institute.

A few years ago, a Peter-like rabbit took up residence in the Gardens but he ended his days squashed flat on the nearby road by a passing car.

So I should feel at home in the Lake District. I was certainly out of sorts as the Lakes 5 picked up after its enforced layoff.

The Thirlmere debacle and the two day break was not what I wanted or needed. Each time we set out geed up for running only to suffer an enforced return to holiday mode. We had two days off, missing out both on competition and our planned rest day programme.

I lost the impetus I had gained over the first two days and set out on Thursday without any great enthusiasm. The biting wind gusting with some force across the high, exposed car park at Caw Hill did nothing to improve matters.

We were going for early starts so it really was a matter of steeling ourselves to get changed and set off on that long walk to the start.

We all wore light anorak tops against the wind, dropping them off at the finish as we passed, and all the while I had one eye on the daunting mountain terrain that lay ahead This was not going to be like our first day run up on the plateau at Swindale. This looked rough and rugged.

The high valleys seemed to house glaciers lipping out and running down the slope. Of course, I knew they were not and that they could not be. They were greyish-green for a start. It all lent to the Alpine atmosphere.

Just how rough, rugged and mountainous the area is was brought home by the first leg.

A quick look at the map shows that the control is a hundred metres or so past the first rocky hill.

I head off down into the valley and towards the hill I see just ahead.

It is only as I get closer that I realised that the massive structure ahead was no more than a knoll on the map and that my hill lies much further on. The eyes can play tricks like that in orienteering. The perspective was wild, everything looking larger than life.

Maybe all the climbs I am fearing are going to be less dramatic than I expect.

So it proved to be.

The first two controls I hit spot on.

The third leg offers the classical choice of over the top or contour round the hillside. Classically too, going over the top or tops gives a safe, easily recognised summit as a first attack point. It is a matter of take a compass bearing and follow it down but down slope location and control finding are always more difficult. That, plus the climb to the top, are the reasons why many people will opt for going round the hill.

However, the contouring option is difficult too. The lie of the land can push you up or down the slope. Deciding how far around you have gone is always problematic, as is finding your attack point.

I opt for contouring and it goes well. I pick off the spurs, maintaining my level until I finally hit a marsh in a large depression. I locate it on the map - easy.

Then things begin to fall apart. I climb over the edge of the basin and run down to the spur ahead and find a crag in the right position, but there is no marker.

My heart sinks. The emotions lie so bare in orienteering.

Perhaps I should have gone for a precise compass bearing. I relocate twice. The second time, I pick up a stream trickling down the slope close to one of the larger valleys, and it directs me into the control. Time has been lost and my rhythm is broken.

Mistakes follow with my technique falling apart as I make too many wrong assumptions and fail to take the time out to consider my mistakes and the best way to resolve them.

The running is excellent. My running is not far short of brilliant – relatively speaking. What looked like glaciers in the valleys from the start turn out to be beds of rushes. I bound over these, bouncing along with an effortless stride. This is certainly my best ever marsh run.

I misread the map and miss number four by a whole hill.

It is almost as if an overnight earthquake had slipped a fault and changed all the angles from those on the map.

To five I pick off each of a series of spurs – Good thinking Bill Man - but then, I forget that I am running low on the spurs and not along their upper edge, turn right and head off down the hill.

I cross a stream but instead of using it as a stopper, I argue that it has been missed from the map and run on.

It's the next lesson for life. It's all too easy to make the facts fit your beliefs rather than building your beliefs on the facts.

I lose a lot of time before I relocate helped by a passing benefactor.

In part, the problem came for losing concentration as I pulled in and passed other runners. Later I notice a recurring pattern to many of my mistakes. A red line on the map joins consecutive control point circles. I seem to be less aware of the map detail to the left of the line than that on the right.

186

I mention this to someone and he immediately asks, "What kind of compass do you use?"

There are two types of compass used regularly in competitive orienteering. The base plate compass has the compass ring set in a rectangular plastic plate. When I used one of these I carried it in my right hand to check the general direction of travel. This gives a rough compass bearing which can be compared with the direction on the map in the other hand.

If a more careful check is needed, the edge of the plate is lined up between the two points on the map – one where you are and the other where you want to be. The needle housing is turned so that its "north" lines line up with the north lines on the map.

If you take it off the map and turn yourself so the needle lies in line with the housing north line, then you are facing the direction you want to go.

The other compass is the thumb compass which has a smaller plastic plate. You carry it on the thumb, usually with the map pinned underneath. The edge runs along the thumb and is permanently kept lined up with the direction of travel on the map. Turning can bring the needle in line with the north lines on the map and automatically brings you into line with the correct direction of travel. The same method can be used for both rough and precise compass work.

The problem with the thumb compass is that unless you change the map from hand to hand part of the detail can be hidden beneath the compass plate and your thumb.

So when I answered, "A thumb compass," he gave a knowing look.

So - that could explain a whole string of route choice errors.

The next day at Helsington Barrows near Kendal again bore this idea out.

To get there, we climbed through the town and out along the old race course road to the limestone heights. It was a really pleasant day with much blue sky and little wind, although what wind there was on the chilly side. Again there was a marvellous panorama on view from the car park.

The limestone combined with many years of sheep grazing has produced a landscape with very few trees, belts of scrub and a deal of short grass. It would be good for running were it not for the stony areas where the limestone has broken through the thin soil and has been eroded and shattered into a surface which can be dangerously unstable underfoot.

Much of it can be seen from the car park and it is obvious from there that there is a lack of shape out there. The contours on the map will be far apart. It will be easy to make mistakes in location and direction. Quality compass and distance management will be at a premium.

The start was within easy reach so I warmed up in the assembly area and felt fit and ready to go when I approached the box.

It was the last day and my previous outings, other than on Day 2 at Guard Wood, were unspectacular to say the least, so there was no pressure to go out and run fast and do well.

Besides we were much more excited for Nicola who was lying second overall in her class and was going out hoping to hold onto that position.

I really did intend to concentrate on getting that perfect run.

I picked up my map and went through my usual routine of taking in the shape of the course and how it fitted into the terrain then lined it up for take off, all the while jogging towards the start marker on the summit of the slight rise ahead. That done, I spent more time than usual on CASH. The control – the far side of a small hill; the attack point – I would wait until I topped the ridge ahead and reached the track to take in the land beyond and decide the best way to cross the rough going in the depression ahead; the stopper - obviously the rising land beyond; the handrail – go on the compass.

This is where I made my first mistake. Again I failed to notice the left of line option which probably was hidden beneath my compass. It turns out that by far the best route to the control would have been a path fifty or so metres away. It circles around the nose of the spur, so avoiding fifteen metres of climb, avoids both the bracken and stony going, and swings back close to the knoll and the control site.

Given four hundred metres of fast going and easy navigation out of an overall six hundred metre run, rather than four hundred metres of rough overland, made it the obvious choice. Apart from anything else, it would have given me the chance to look at the routes to the next two controls, and what is more important, still time to settle in to the map and the terrain.

It proved to be an expensive mistake. By the time I bridge the spur and reach the path on top, after ploughing through an area of rough gorse and bracken, I have been thrown off line and I am deep in the pre second wind trough and I have lost the edge of my concentration.

I look at the map and pick out the deep if small valley running alongside the control site.

I look across the depression and pick out a valley and from where I stand can see a control in it.

Of course, if it is my control it should not be in the valley. It would be hidden behind a nearby knoll.

The mind under stress does not think that way.

Instead it jumps to the conclusion that it is my control and that the best way to get to it is to head to the right, briefly following the path until it comes time to head into some of the thicket style grot on the hillside.

I duly struggle my way through and arrive at the control to suffer the customary disappointment when I discover it is not mine.

Fortunately I relocate quickly and head in the right direction to remedy my error, skirting round the depression until I hit a point of easy access to the knoll and nail it. I have covered six hundred metres of really hard going and taken at least twice as long as I might have done.

It crossed my mind in the days that followed that instead of concentrating on CASH, I should use COACH as my technique acronym – Control, Options, taking in all possible routes to an Attack point, noting the Catching feature which will act as the stopper, and the Handrail features found along the selected route option.

"Options" would include making sure nothing was hidden under my compass.

On the way to three, I discover the path system on the map bears scant resemblance to what is on the ground.

These "animal" paths come and go, and usually migrate across an area.

The vegetation mapping too suffers from amorphism. Little looks as it should.

Number four should be easy – a crag in a gully, in a bit of woodland.

The vegetation line I follow merges with others and I overshoot off to the left and more time is lost.

This is turning into a nightmare.

Number five only serves to consolidate that conclusion. I play it safe, deciding not to take the straight line and compass approach, seek the path to the left instead, find and follow it. (You see, I'm learning). Follow it and count off the paths that cross it as I go. That's the plan.

All it takes is to have one extra unmarked, grassy path crossing right to left for everything to be thrown into disarray. Instead of concentrating on reaching the top of the hill and a major path junction just before it, I turn of early to go off on what was always destined to be a fruitless search.

Catching sight of a distant rock that is control six helps me out of yet another time wasting predicament. I find five and six is easy.

From then on, despite a couple of wavers, I run well and run on target.

I pick up a dozen or more places but it is too late to make up for earlier stupidity.

Catastrophe, not real catastrophe, merely sporting catastrophe, but catastrophe nonetheless.

Sports writers have a tendency to use hyperbole – catastrophe, tragic.

Let's face it, while sports people, like anyone else, can find themselves in tragic circumstances, with few exceptions it never happens on the pitch or track or, in the case of orienteering, in the forest. I can remember stopping myself in full flow as I dictated a couple of hundred words of copy down the phone to one newspaper or another.

"No, change that," I told the copy taker. "This is not 'tragic'. It is athletics we are talking about. Let's say 'disappointing'."

As I sprint down the finish lane, fellow Scot Alan catches me and I move over when he asks me to let him by. Not only is he ten years younger than me, he always was faster.

"Not bad for a couple of old men," he says as we go to download.

Not bad at the end of a not so good day.

Nicola also suffered a "disaster" but kept her second place, so we left the Lakes Five with something to celebrate.

Looking back, I now think I went to the Lake District poorly prepared.

I moved up an age class to take the pressure off and be able to concentrate on my prime objective of scoring a perfect run. I "carry a lot of baggage" as the saying goes when it comes to running in the Lake District, with many runs I prefer to forget, so maybe I didn't go there and run with the confidence needed.

Then again, I knew the week would be dominated by moorland events but I had not done the wide open, big vista training I needed to make the switch from forest competition. That was not a matter of choice. There are very few moorland areas mapped to orienteering standard in my locality. Furthermore, while I had planned to make best use of what is available, my ankle and back injuries had cut short the opportunity. I'd had no wish to go too far off the beaten track, miles from my car, just in case my injury might catch me out.

You make your decisions and take your choice.

[Lakes 5 maps and courses - http://www.routegadget.co.uk – Appendix 1; item (n)]

26

Our Lakes stay over, we headed for Yorkshire where Nicola's club was staging its traditional British autumn season opener, the White Rose Weekend, starting Saturday morning.

Would this open up my chances of scoring a perfect run?

It seemed unlikely.

In orienteering, the area is famed, or should that be notorious, for its steep valleys biting deep into the moors and wolds. The moors themselves, unlike those in the Lake District, are largely featureless, covered in deep heather and offer little by way of orienteering terrain.

The rest of the open land, is largely farming fields.

The valleys and in some cases the land between, are wooded, mainly with coniferous plantations, and it is the best of these areas which are used by local orienteering club Eborienteers – a pun based on the Roman name for York, "Ebor".

Any orienteering courses here usually contain stretches of thick forest and steep climb with much path route choice to avoid these. While navigating between the points is usually easy, control site location - close to the control or "within the circle" as it is described - is often tricky.

Running to perfection would be tough in places, needing much concentration, and concentration spent there would leave less for focusing on markers. Concentration on its own would not be enough. I would need to switch it at a moment's notice between running, the going underfoot, the visibility through the trees, the map, the terrain features, and my changing handrail. It would be very different from Lake District, Hungary, and the other British areas I had competed and trained on during the season to date.

The White Rose weekend is different from other multi day events of its kind.

First it is organised by just one club rather than a partnership. These are common on the continent; the events we went to near Krakow and Uslar were run by the local club. They are less run of the mill in Britain where usually three or more clubs come together for bigger weekend events.

Second, like many of the continental events, they include a variety of minor subsidiary events in their programme, including mountain bike orienteering, a sprint and a hill race.

Lastly, it is centred on the event camp site. Most multi day events have a camp site but few use it as the event centre and few can claim that the camping is almost as important to the atmosphere and ambiance as the orienteering itself.

That reputation has brought problems and the orienteering press and websites has long carried tales of conflict across the generations with older campers complaining that youngsters have ruined the weekend with late night revelling in the dark, while teenagers retaliate with complaints that the wrinklies are joy killers who should shut up or get out of this youngsters world.

The war ended with the youth wing accepting partial segregation, occupying a far corner of the camping field where they can party the night away if they so choose. However, once there, without the opposition of their elders to force them out on a limb, they usually choose not to.

Now, not just now but always, camping has never been one of my favourite pastimes. Forget lying on the ground, or at best on an air or frame bed. Where else can you spend your night yo-yoing between sleep and wide eyed wakefulness and yet still end up sliding out the door before sun rise? You never, never, never get a flat place to pitch a tent. Then there is the crawling - crawling into bed, crawling out of bed, crawling to get dressed, crawling to get changed, crawling to find your shoes, crawling to find your towel, crawling to find your torch. When else do you spend so many cramped painful hours living in each others pockets?

Then there is washing and the washing up facilities "What facilities?" I hear you asking.

What's fun about standing in the rain washing up greasy plates in lukewarm water? We go camping and all of a sudden we throw away all the basic rules of hygiene; the rules we worshiped before leaving our far off, comfy homes; the rules which separate modern first world living from a third world struggle for existence.

Worst of all, there are the treks to the "rest rooms", usually some sort of truck delivered "loo". The long trek made in the wet and possibly the dark, slipping in the mud which ends up coating everything.

Go camping in Britain and three things happen. It rains. The wind gets up. Temperatures slump. This is no way to take a break unless you're a masochist.

I can remember three great camping masochism moments in my life.

Two of these took place on our Great Western Isles journey.

On Lewis, the largest and furthest out of the Hebrides, we camped by one of the many idyllic beaches on the island.

Spectacularly, the local council had supplied a small toilet block with hot water laid on. There was only one other family there, in a caravan.

We were in a large, metal-framed tent we had bought second hand.

On the second night the wind rose and gradually built up to gale force.

Into the night, every gust threatened to lift the tent and dump it in the sea. At around two in the morning my fears of disaster forced me to get up and hold onto the frame in a bid to stop it taking off while the canvas buffeted, bulged and buckled under the force of what was an almighty wind. There was I hanging on with all my strength while jumping from one side of the tent to another.

It must have been 4am before I felt it safe to slump back into bed and grab a few hours sleep before morning.

Surprisingly, the children slept through it all.

Next morning, in the surrealist calm that often follows such storms, the tent was still standing.

The horizontal aluminium tubes in the frame showed the full effects of my wrestling match with the gale. They were bent, not exactly buckled, but sizeably bent out of shape and – they would never recover.

A few days later we had sailed to Skye on our way home and pitched our tent at a site in the attractive capital of the island, Portree.

After a first rain-drenched night, everything was damp and soggy as we got up, and after a rudimentary breakfast we bundled ourselves into the car and set off to see the sights.

The scenery on Skye is dramatic as well as beautiful, an awe inspiring mixture of sea, sky, cliffs, beaches, moorland and mountains strung along the narrow twisting strands of road.

Highland roads can prove a bit of a problem to visitors. Passing places cause more consternation and nervous disorders amongst the uninitiated than any city centre traffic jam.

Two sure signs show up members of the tourist battalions, the sub 20mph crawl and the headlong dive across your bows to reach the right hand side passing place to let your approaching car by.

In recent years, European Community funding has built a number of quality roads on Skye.

If you want to see what Britain has got out of the European Union, go to Skye.

Back in the bad old days, we were wending our way along the bad old roads, rain teaming down to wipe out all sight of anything beyond the dykes and fences by the road side.

The mighty Cuillin Mountains with their sky searching peaks were no doubt there but they were invisible.

What a day! What an island tour! What a car drive, wet and miserable outside; three miserable children and two miserable parents steaming up the windows inside. The landscape was a dismal and unmitigated curtain of grey.

At the end of the afternoon, the campsite driveway was a welcome sight.

Relief!

It didn't last long.

The sight of the campsite ended that.

Everywhere, uncharted highland burns had sprung up on the slopes beyond and were heading for the sea right through our field. A salmon running up stream to its spawning ground would not have surprised me. One torrent, small but a torrent nonetheless, ran right through our tent. The camp was in uproar. Tents were being torn down as people made their escape. It seemed the right thing to do, but escape to where? The whole island was a marsh and so would be much of the mainland beyond even if a ferry berth were available.

What could we do? Who could we turn to?

Give the islanders their due they were there for us that day.

The tourist office was open and fully operational although it was well past closing time. The staff were working double time, phoning around to find accommodation, and not always in guest houses or B&Bs. They were full already. Families across the island were opening their homes to take in the needy like ourselves.

We ended up on a farming, fishing croft about five miles away. Not only did they give us beds for the night. There were hot baths for all, our clothes were laid out to dry in front of the fire, and in the morning we were served up a full highland fry up breakfast with tea and toast before we went on our way.

My third tale of camping catastrophe dates back to our days in Africa.

One holiday, we drove the eight hundred odd miles from our base in Kenya to the Murchison Falls National Park in Uganda.

The park was rich in wildlife.

We saw lion for the first time. If you really want to appreciate the wild in wildlife look a lion in the eyes. Not any old lion, but one in its natural outdoor habitat where everything it looks at, including you, is weighed up as a likely meal.

We saw possibly the biggest bull elephant in the world, one of many monsters.

Every now and then, a bull elephant, a bit like stallions do, lets down its penis. Usually it is held up inside a sheath out of harm's way.

As we watched in amazement, this monster let loose its monster. Still flaccid, it grew longer and longer until it seemed in danger of touching and rubbing along the ground. The beast or nature was up to this. It hitched it up, putting a kink or double bend in it to keep it out of harm's way.

The Nile, which emerges from Lake Victoria to flow north to the Mediterranean Sea near Alexandria, goes through the park and boat trips ran up river to take in the Murchison Falls.

The banks were lined with the most huge crocodiles while countless hippos swam in the pools and paraded on the sand banks.

It was a memorable experience.

We were camping, as were our friends.

Now to you it might seem the height of stupidity to camp in a wild life park which had more animated death dealing devices than a horror film, but the parks all supplied camp sites with sheltered cooking areas and toilets – dry, long drop, hole in the ground toilets it is true, but all with a measure of privacy and not too smelly.

Besides the rooms at the park hotel and admin centre were very expensive.

Now this might not be the hottest place on earth, but it is certainly the hottest I have been to. It is a massive basin which is part of the Rift Valley which stretches thousands of miles to Lake Malawi to the South and it sits at a much lower altitude than most of Uganda and much of Kenya.

It was so hot that we rose early each day, the tent already heating up to furnace temperatures, breakfasted quickly, jumped into the car and drove off looking for "game".

There was no "air-con" in cars in those days but with the windows open there was enough of a breeze to ensure survival.

At night, the heat continued, but the tent was always kept fastened up as the campsite attracted many animals searching for food scraps.

You could hear them, and if you were absolutely forced by a beer or two too many to take a trip in the night, you could see their eyes shining in the beam of the torch. It was scary stuff.

The news board at the park centre carried these stories of how park rangers had been attacked by lions while they lay in their tents at night.

One man had escaped out the door while the lion climbed in a window at the back. It was a big tent. There was a picture of it.

Another was grabbed by the shoulder by another lion which squeezed under the edge of the canvas, but managed to free himself and get away. That's a tale for him to tell the grandchildren.

197

Our tent was an old fashioned canvas, ridge tent – what was called an officer's tent - which we bought at a shop in Nairobi where we paid extra to have a ground sheet sown in.

We thought that would keep any snakes and creepy crawlies out.

After a few days we went on by ourselves to the Queen Elizabeth Park to the South where after a day of touring the magnificent crater lake country we headed for the camp site.

I suppose we should have asked questions when we found we were the only people camping there.

After feeding and sitting out for a while we duly bedded down.

I woke up first with a commotion some way off. A shot was fired and there was a deal of shouting. We learned next day that an elephant had made an all out foraging attack on the park hotel area and had to be scared off.

The next time I awoke, Katharine was shaking my shoulder.

"There's something there," she whispered.

We sat stock still straining our ears and sure enough we could hear it.

An animal sniffing. Maybe it was just imagination but it sounded like a big animal sniffing.

I reached with one hand to check that the rope ties used to close the front of the tent were all in place and with the other I picked up the builders hammer we used to knock in the tent pegs.

There it was again.

Sniffing and then, horror of horrors, the beast was scratching at the canvas wall of the tent!

Once, twice maybe three or four times came the sound of claws on canvas. We were too petrified even to hang onto each other. I had my builder's hammer ready. I was going to make it fight for its dinner.

It came again. We had obviously fired its interest.

Then it went away. Just like that it was gone. No sound of feet tramping off through the grass or quietening snorts of disgust as it got further away. Just silence. We waited. Nothing. It had left. Maybe it didn't like the smell of sweat, the sweat of fear.

The next morning we went too. At first light we packed up, keeping an eye open for the approach of any marauding wildlife, said good bye to our African camping adventure and headed for the nearest town.

Well, of course, camping in Yorkshire was nothing like that.

It was more in the familiar British style, cold, damp and windy, or is it only when I go camping it is like that?

We were up on the edge of the North York Moor about three miles from the popular tourist village of Helmsley.

Tents were pitched in a large field surrounded by woods which was probably just as well for the winds on Saturday and Sunday were quite ferocious.

We were joined by our four year old grandson Andrew as well as Nicola. Since Ebor is her club she had to take an early shift at the drinking water station in the forest.

We drove up on the Saturday morning and after helping to set up the tent and taking a light lunch, I changed and set off for my 12.20 start.

Coming at the end of a week of running I had decided away back in June to opt for shorter courses in Yorkshire and run my own age group. That meant less distance but more social pressure. Roger – the Day 1 winner at the JK - was on the start list.

Up at the start there was a stiff, cold wind blowing but it was bright and sunny. On the other hand, there were distant showers, thick black curtains littering the horizon in almost very direction. We were being lucky.

So, to get on with it, White Rose, Day 1, control one is easy. A run along the path then duck into the forest on the left and run along and down the slope to catch the gully and find the marker. Great. I take 2m51s – just two-seconds down on Roger.

The path run from the start had given every chance to look at the map and take in the course.

Number two, a tree stump, lies downhill near the valley bottom. I opt for the path run, longer but easier going underfoot than going directly. One of the passing showers, a cold, short, sharp shower with big, fat drops not far removed from hail caught me out in the open but I shrugged it off.

I clock 5m19s. Roger, who took the direct forest route, was 46 seconds slower.

After that it was Roger all the way. I hold my own on the open field runs, edging him on three more legs and tying him at 23 seconds on the run in. Interestingly we often opt for the same routes.

Elsewhere he leaves me for dead. Am I being more hesitant or is he just faster on rougher going and up the hills?

I make minor errors, veering too far to the left to avoid a dangerous looking crag at number three and lose two minutes. I misread the control ID number at four and waver badly before dibbing.

I make errors. At number six confusion reigns as I make a 180 degree error just outside the circle, before collecting on a chance fence. I lose one and half minutes more.

So this was not a perfect run but apart from number six there were no real mistakes and I was running well all the way even if Roger was running faster. I had come close. I could come closer the next day.

[See map and course at: http://www.routegadget.co.uk – Appendix 1; item (o)]

27

No way is orienteering a fair sport. I don't just mean there are blokes out there who can thrash me. That sort of thing is what any sport is about. When it comes to things physical we are not all born equal.

I don't mean the sometimes faulty planning. The best courses are built around navigation features which lead to each control, with maybe a bit of short distance compass work needed to close in on the marker.

If the site is deep into thick "fight" forest, or bracken, it becomes a bingo control; it is chance if you find it, the more so if it is a hollow rather than a knoll or boulder.

Again, the marker can be hidden behind a fallen tree or a boulder for competitors on one route but not another. That is unfair.

No, when I say unfair I mean the things built into the very nature of the sport. Some will find a deer track while others will not. In chaotic running some will find the easier going through the brashings others won't. Some will find tracks leading directly towards or even into the control site, tracks which were not there before. As few as a dozen people running through thick ground cover can be enough to make these "elephant tracks" as they are called.

Day 2 of the White Rose, I am first out. So what? So first out means you're the trail blazer. If you are the leader of a big pack the back markers will have a new path to follow from start to finish. Head a smaller field and you won't be making paths, but you and the other early runners break down the bracken and flag up the entry and exit points from any track runs.

A quick look at the map shows it is reasonably flat going at the start with few contours to follow before the course heads into one of those steep valleys. Much path running with the problem of finding the right place to plunge into the woods.

Number one offers a simple route choice, for the path splits in two forming a V-shape and the control is a hundred or so metres further on in the forest almost exactly between them. It is on a dry ditch.

I take another look at the map. Noticing that a band of thicker forest – a strip of light green on map – skirts the left hand path, I opt for the one on the right. That's a mistake. There is every chance the all pervasive bracken will be less thick in the darker wood.

As it is, after a hundred metres or so I turn off the path and find I am burrowing into bracken that is both thick and chest high.

Next I find there are a number of ditches in the wood that are not on the map. The mapper has opted to mark only the two deeper ditches. Besides any ditch is going to be difficult to see in this vegetation.

I burrow on through to no effect, until I finally decide to make for the path on the other side.

I make it but where exactly am I? I opt now to relocate from a path junction just ahead and use that as my attack point. What I took at a glance to be a north south running path turns out to be one of the magnetic north lines.

Back I go again until I see the start kite ahead and then judging the distance along the path go in. I find the ditch but still find some difficulty in following it to the marker.

That's over six minutes gone when I should have done it in less than two.

All chance of a perfect run has been blown away of course.

A reasonably competitive run is still on the cards for everyone can make a mistake in this sort of featureless going.

So two is spot on; I waver at three; struggle through the brashings on the way to four before finding an unmapped path in the supposedly thick vegetation which proves a big help. It runs along a fence and is most likely a well used animal track.

By this time my orienteering is going to pieces and I'm reduced to seat of the pants navigating.

Five, six and seven, go by and I'm running with a small pack and they all seem to know what they are doing in this fairly shapeless sort of forest.

Maybe they are more used to it than I am. English orienteers have a terrain advantage competing in England.

Leaving seven – a couple of posts and a stretch of wire, all that is left of a defunct fence - I take control of myself, head the others into number eight and leave them on the way to number nine.

Then we hit the steep valley that dominates the map for the first time.

Number ten is a re-entrant along its edge, an area of complex shapes, difficult going and low visibility.

I go in from the start of a strip of roadside clearing, but then it gets tough. In this difficult going, the first we have really come across this weekend, the problem is getting into the mapper's mind and seeing how they saw the shapes. I hit a re-entrant but it is empty. I should have aimed off target and followed the line of dips and knolls along.

Now, I go back along the slope edge some twenty metres. That re-entrant is empty too, but this one is really the space between two little hills on the map so I use this as my starting point to take in the features along the slope.

On to the next. It's not this one. I have been here already so on to the next again. It should be here and sure enough it is.

The map shows open running but the trees in this fairly typical plantation have the relatively young larch close together and they have branches that scratch at skin and clothes as I carry on from one re-entrant to the next to find eleven. Got it too.

After that I lose another minute. My concentration is waning. A hurried glance at the map proves my undoing. I go out onto the road thinking I have to cross it only to find that twelve is an easy feature just a hundred metres through the wood from where I was. I have to come back in to get it.

Next it is off along a path for three hundred metres or so to thirteen. Easy. It can't be that easy. It isn't. The path is a bit down the slope and it is a broken path on different levels and the woods about it are really thick and unforgiving. I plough on.

Sigi, the Swedish man who started just behind me is there as well. He must have made mistakes too. I hit thirteen before him and, with the trees opening up, opt to go through the woods to fourteen.

Fine intentions but the terrain along with my determined bid to avoid the slope, pushes me off line and I find myself back at the forest road. No worry, I pick up the edge of the pine woods ahead and go in from there to find the clearing and the control marker sitting at its far end.

That leaves four more to go. It's almost over. Will I be glad? Any one of these past four controls could have proved crucial in deciding the winner that day. They were that testing. Out there far from view is where the competition is being decided.

One of the difficulties in covering orienteering for the press, be it newspapers or magazines, is finding the real stories.

Covering athletics you see the stories happen there in front of you on the track. If nothing great in story terms happens there you might search around, interview the athlete or his coach and see if there is a background story you can use to hinge your piece.

Often you can go along just to cover one event, the 100m say, watch, interview, get your story angle, write it up and that's it over.

In orienteering, all the action is background action. It is all taking place out of sight out there in the woods, or nowadays, in the urban sprint streets. A sprint finish to a chasing start race might give you some live action but otherwise you have to delve and dig out your story. I have spent a great deal of time at orienteering events interviewing runners to see if they had a story to tell. They didn't always get the idea and often there was no big story.

A disappointed pre-event favourite was always a good starting point. Sometimes I would pick up something in other runners' gossip but you have to work for your living as a journalist in orienteering, waiting around for two to three hours, chatting with people after they cross the line and before they drive off home. I remember approaching one newspaper sub-editor to see if I could interest him in a British

Championship piece. "Get back to me if someone breaks a leg," he said speaking metaphorically.

No "break a leg" story came bigger than Britain's World gold medal Relay win in Olomouc in 2008.

Jamie Stevenson was fighting it out at the front on the final leg against Gueorgiou, and the Frenchman seemed to be getting away as the British runner found he had a slightly longer leg after a near to finish control.

In relays, I would point out, all three laps cover the same courses, and all teams do the same three course overall. On any one lap, runners may find they are visiting different controls from other runners around them.

As I say, the Frenchman seemed to have made a crucial break but that, as it turned out, was academic.

Gueorgiou sucked a bee into his mouth as he ran along.

It stung him in the throat as he swallowed it, and as his throat swelled up he found himself gasping for breath. He was out of the race. He walked back to the arena where a helicopter arrived to take him to hospital

Stevenson, unaware of the drama ran home to win.

To get back to Yorkshire with number fourteen behind me, I am heading now for a big area of open runnable woodland at the end of a long path trek. At least that is what the map tells me. As I hit the path I can see the big open pine wood far ahead on the left hand side

The kilometre long path run is tough going – uphill and that stiff wind is blowing right into my face.

I throttle back a little to keep aerobic and keep on running. Looking forward to the forest run ahead helps to keep me going.

It is with nothing short of relief I get there and clamber through the thick vegetation and forestry debris that lines the track. I am really looking forward to the two hundred metres or so through the big pines when I leave this grot behind me.

I wait in vain.

I can only think that the mapper looked at the wood and saw what seemed to be easy running heather and never really tried to cross it.

The grotty going continues, on and on and on without mercy. I am pushed off course, stumbling and tripping through hip high heather, over trunks and branches which at every step threaten to break a leg.

It is so exhausting. I am staggering as I reach the marker.

However, there is no respite.

The next is more of the same, with a more trickily placed marker into the bargain, hiding down beside a well disguised tree stump. Sweat is streaming down my forehead into my eyes. I can hardly see.

By the time I leave that one behind, I'm going round in circles and so is my head.

I am holding the map the wrong way round so I start out along the wrong track and have to double back.

I misread the contours around seventeen and struggle offline going up hill through heather I might have avoided.

Sigi catches and passes me.

I lose four minutes on my top rivals at number sixteen and four more at seventeen.

I can barely run the uphill finish and come home with a dismal time of 70m24s. Despite losing three minutes at number ten, Roger clocked under sixty. I had lost eight minutes of the deficit struggling along between fifteen and seventeen.

Over the two days of competition he was the easy overall winner of our group. Strangely, I might say shockingly, I came second. What was everyone else up to?

The prize giving was held that evening in the campsite marquee before we all got together for a barbecue.

Barbecue and camping – a fatal combination. Well, of course the weather was windy, a bit wet and cold - but nobody seemed to mind.

[See map and course at: http://www.routegadget.co.uk – Appendix 1; item (p)]

28

The summer multi days over it was into the autumn season, and while November still seemed a long way off I was beginning to feel a bit apprehensive. There were many events on the calendar but if I didn't buckle down there might just not be enough.

My running was improving with both the uphill stretches and the rough terrain feeling easier as I found my running technique adapting to the conditions. My navigation was still likely to fall apart and I regularly ditched any attempt at regimented technique under pressure or during a dip in concentration.

Time was not yet running out but it was getting scarce.

The theory is that time goes by faster as you get older.

How many find that looking back on the year, or the decade just past everything seems to have gone so quickly? Is it a case of familiarity breeding boredom, with one year at work and home very like another, with nothing to make the days stand out on their own? I always say that if you want a long weekend then start using it on Friday night. Overlapping the weekend into Monday makes it even longer and by Monday night, Friday night seems a long, long way away but then into the humdrum of work or home again, and the next weekend comes up fast.

Conversely, go for a two week break somewhere new, and a couple of weeks meeting new people, visiting new places, eating new food, doing something different every day, and a fortnight seems like a month.

I've got to say that time never went faster than when I was teaching. Each day in the classroom is sliced up by ringing bells into forty minute slots. Each week is a repeat of the one before. Each year has the same lessons, same exams, same days, same weeks, same terms, just like last year.

Little or nothing changes to mark the passage of time.

Everyone lives from one weekend to the next and looks forward to the next holiday, all wishing their lives away.

Out on my own and into journalism each day was different. Of course there was repetition: preview stories before the weekend, weekend action, Monday backup stories, midweek interest items. In addition, there was the non-sport stuff, advertising write ups, court stories, the occasional feature piece and much ringing around to sell my ideas, working to expand my market place.

Then there were the big sports events, everything from national to world championships, with all the travelling, meeting new people, the buzz of interviews and finding a story. Often, with a number of different articles to write up for different papers, sometimes from different countries, it would mean finding several story lines – writing them all up and getting everything out to the customers on time.

Over the years, as the job and the work became more familiar, time began to go faster again.

It is nothing to do with getting old. It is all to do with variety.

Of course when you are young, everything is new. Everything offers so much variety.

I can remember when anything scheduled for two or three months ahead, like exams, were so far away they hardly seemed worth consideration. Nowadays two or three months time seems just around the corner. Last year seems like yesterday, although I can't remember everything about it. Next year looms large almost before the New Year has begun. It moves slowly into January then February, but by March it is speeding up and summer is almost upon us. Hit July and, as some folks say, the nights are drawing in; after all it is getting dark before midnight again.

As I look out my window, the oaks on Craig Hill are a patchwork of yellows and browns, shining golden in the afternoon sun, with great black crevices of shadow between them. They all leaf and cast at slightly different times to produce this colour patchwork. The big tree standing above the river at the bottom of our road is the last to burst into leaf and the last to lose them. It is still green.

On Craig a'Barns, the larches are a paler shade of yellow and paler still is the spread of birches and the grass between on the flanks of Newtyle.

The first frost is surely just around the corner and yet it seems that despite our travels and some glorious summer days the winter is not long gone. Of course it stayed a long time into spring this year with snow on the ground into April. So if I exercise my mind and think back to this time last year and dwell momentarily on all the things that have happened in between then it does seem a long time ago.

Now retired, I try to avoid doing the same thing every day and every week, avoid living by a well filled diary to leave room for the occasional surprise, and it works. Time is slowing down again.

However, if that is the case, then as August slipped surreptitiously into September, it was not slowing insofar as it prevented the feeling that the end of the season was coming up fast and the fixtures running out.

On the first Sunday in September the National League opened its autumn series at Birsemore Forest back on Deeside just outside Aboyne.

What a lovely piece of conifer forest this is with large areas of widely spread pine and larches but the rocky slopes just above the finish and the descent tested my technique.

Dithering, standing looking at the map and the terrain round about me, going nowhere or nowhere fast, is one of my major faults and it cost me much time at Birsemore.

Neil - he comes from Aberdeen - is one of my major rivals. He is currently running up in a younger age group, but next year or the year after when he moves up to join me, then I can say good bye to my championship titles.

However, if he is a rival of mine, I can't claim to be one of his major rivals for I cannot remember when I last put him under pressure let alone beat him.

Years ago when we ran over longer courses with longer "legs" I may have taken his scalp on one or two occasions. Back then, I may not have been running as well as I do now but I was running faster, if you can see the difference. I can run more efficiently now with more rhythm, more enjoyment but back then I had a longer stride and the strength of a younger man. A decade or so ago a research physiologist at Houston University noticed that a number of former student "guinea pigs" were still living in the area in their early fifties. Some were working at the university with him.

Training around Dunkeld - you've never had it so good

Forest running in the Craig a'Barns foothills. (K Melville)

In the forest cathedral - my favourite trail, the Hermitage circuit. (K Melville)

Twelve of them agreed to take part in a backup experiment designed to compare their fitness thirty odd years down the line, measuring their VO2 max – their ability to use up oxygen while exercising to exhaustion.

Some were in regular training. Others were couch potatoes but all took up a twelve week training routine designed to get them to maximum fitness.

Then they were tested. To everyone's surprise, their VO2 max results were the same as they had been all those years before.

Not surprisingly, none of them could perform to the same level physically as they had done as twenty year olds.

One factor recognised as possibly influencing this was that all were carrying more weight than in their physical heyday.

Possibly too, despite their recent training, none had that spring in their step. As I have already said, somewhere down the line that elasticity has been lost.

The muscles are stretched as happens when the foot lands and takes your weight. The elasticity helps absorb the impact. The energy is released as the muscle prepares to contract and does so lending a spring to the take off.

Ever since you hit that mid-forties watershed that spring has been on the wane.

Pace counting is the orienteering technique used to measure how far you have gone towards the control, an attack point or other route feature. When I took up the sport in my mid-thirties I could measure a hundred metres along a path with, as I recall, thirty strides, fewer if I was pushing the pace. Now, I take thirty-seven, forty even if the path is slightly broken or on the soft side. My stride is shorter and consequently I run more slowly.

There is a riverside path in Birnam which runs from along by the A9 main road, under the old Telford built bridge and all the way to the fishing hut at the start of Murthly estate. Seven years ago when we moved to live here I started using a nine hundred metre or so stretch for end of training run time trials. Usually after a run up by the Hermitage or Craigvinean I would hit the watch as I turned onto the path and stop it at my turnoff for home.

I was unfit at the time following a long break from regular running due to a long standing achilles problem and I was on a two pill per day beta blocker programme.

My best time saw the clock stop at 3m20s. My objective was to get it down below three minutes.

However, I have never done it. I doubt if I ever will. I have come off beta blockers all together with no ill affects, I might add, and I have vastly superior fitness. Despite all that, I am lucky now to break 3m40s on a good day.

Nothing works quite as it used to. Back when the body parts were working better I could run faster and further, take on courses more suited to my strengths.

Back thirty years ago, not only were the courses longer but, mile for mile there were fewer controls – maybe fifteen over eight kilometres compared with fifteen over five now. As I climbed the age groups this change in control number to distance ratio was my downfall in competitive terms. I lose too much time "in the circle" or, as Birsemore showed, looking about me like a grazing deer, questioning the terrain in between the circles.

Let's ignore the first leg. By design I started out slowly, getting into the map and the distance. I crossed a small heathery hill and still using the map regularly dropped into the valley beyond and followed it down to the marker. Neil took a detour round the hill and crossed a small marsh but he was obviously moving in his usual go-get-it way and he bettered my three minute timing by all of sixteen-seconds.

Number two and I was still on for a perfect run as I set out following a long meandering marsh which left a fifty metre run from a forest road into the next small valley control site.

What I wasn't to know was that it was heavy, wet going underfoot in this marsh, and the chilly water was deeper in places than I expected, forcing me to slow down to pick my way over it on tufts of grass and rushes.

Again I had failed to notice the left hand route over the marsh to a track that went all the way to the same attack point. Maybe my thumb compass was in the way. Neil took 1m20s out of me going that longer way round.

To number three we both went exactly the same way but I was marginally to the right of the crucial path junction right by a cottage, as I came out of the first stretch of forest. It's odd how something more or less unusual, like a cottage in the middle of a wood, can make you slacken your stride just for a moment and make you look at your map again. Somehow Neil still took another fifteen-seconds out of me. Where?

Number four gave the answer. (There was Trish just ahead. She started two minutes before me). It was a really tough leg across a slope that dipped and dived, throwing up little hills and dropping into little valleys. It was rough but the control, a big boulder, was relatively easy so it was a matter of running all out to the second and larger strip of open ground which ran down the slope, following it down to go back into the wood and hit the boulder.

That was what Neil did, covering the four hundred metres and checking out his map on the way, in ten-seconds under four minutes. Remember we are talking really rough cross-country here, and these times are not to be compared with road or track running times. The fastest out that day, both in their twenties, covered a similar leg on the same stretch in under two minutes.

Unbelievably, I took over seven minutes after often pausing to identify where I was, asking myself, is this that valley on the map and is this that "ride", looking through the trees; asking myself is that the big clearing I'm looking for, instead of just getting there and getting there fast.

Trying too hard not to make a mistake is a mistake.

It is all too easy to forget the Gueorgiou technique of concentrating on the landmark features.

I left control number four still on track for a mistake free run, but was it costing me time? Was I navigating too carefully, always trying to know where I was, to avoid a blunder and so letting my running fall below perfection level?

I squeeze through the fence at the bottom of the hill and onto the path beyond.

A hundred metres further as I passed cottage corner again, my mind did a flip.

Remember what I said – paths look so easy on a course and you can certainly run faster on them but they can suck you in to thinking the navigation is easy and letting your concentration slip.

Just for a moment I think again about number four. Think on catching Tricia and leaving her behind.

That concentration slip leaves just enough brain space to let a mistake slip in. My mind misses a step, and suddenly as I turn the corner I wonder, "Am I going the right way?" I juggle the map around and see that almost certainly I have made a one hundred and eighty degree error. I turn and run back.

"We're going the wrong way, Trish," I shout as I run by.

"No, we're not," she shouts after me.

"What?"

I stop and catch her up.

"You were right," she says and points to the map.

Curses, that's my perfect run gone.

Still cursing under my breath I get running again and soon leave Trish behind me. I am running well now. I feel a spring in my step and I can up the cadence and hold it all together.

Forcing myself to forget my blunder I forge on.

Two hundred metres and I cross the stream; two hundred more and I leave the path, turning into the wood to follow a broad ride. I am in the best of the forest now, big forty year old spruce trees smelling of the best of nature's incense. It gives you a heady feeling, makes the nose tingle.

An animal path runs up the ride, so although I'm running further that the straight line route, it should be faster. I think about running, pushing my knees forward, holding my foot horizontal, picking up my heels. "Yes, I've got rhythm."

Then I hesitate. I can see a marker off to the left and it is in a valley.

"Is it mine?" I ask myself. Of course I should know it isn't. I have to cross the next small rise to find my re-entrant, but just to be sure I turn into the wood and start running towards it.

"Stop", I shout at myself. "Look at the map."

Of course it isn't mine. My one is further over, over the next spur.

I force myself to go there, but I have lost time.

One, I have left the path too early and lost some of my advantage.

Two, now I have to run further over the rough forest floor.

Taking in the delights of the forest and all this thinking about running is costing me dear.

The control is over the next spur. Two or three of us run into it together.

Neil, who opted for a forest run over the final two hundred metres takes another thirty-seconds out of me.

Heading for number six we go exactly the same way, climbing the ride to cross the top of the hill and then turn into the right when we see a wall crossing the ride about fifty metres ahead.

Then I slow. The terrain has taken me by surprise. It is a rougher little hill that I expected, and the crag I am after is further down and further off to the right than I imagined.

Neil doesn't do that and chalks up another half minute.

Heading for seven I go out to the wall and follow it until veering off down a valley to find the crag. I have a minor problem finding the wall because it is broken down just at this point. I circle back quickly to find it further along. Fine run. Good control. I beat Neil by two-seconds on exactly the same line. So you see I can run as fast as he does.

One look at number eight on the map and you can see it is a toughie, a boulder in a group of four, the one furthest west. However, there are many other boulders around and many confusing contour shapes.

I should take it carefully.

I am tempted to follow the girl just ahead. She is a good orienteer.

She is also a good runner and I can see that I'm never going to keep up with her on the initial uphill stretch.

We reach a big marsh with me still running just behind her. I can see it on the map.

I am still arguing with myself whether I should go over the top or round the hill when I hit a big timber drag-out lane going off to the right.

I make a snatch decision to go round to the right, but while I had been heading for the top of the hill with another smaller hill on the down slope beyond to act as my attack point, now I have no distinct features in mind.

As I breast the rise I turn left to circle round that side of the hill.

Then I hit a large marsh. I've got it on the map. I climb round it and head along the slope on a rough compass bearing.

Everything is going well I assure myself, but without conviction. I am jittery. I don't like this. I am closer to the summit than I expected.

I have forgotten my small hill attack point.

I chalk off a big open valley to the left and then hit on a massive boulder.

That should be it, a careful compass bearing and a walk in should take me to the control.

My brain is somewhere six feet above my head again jiving around like some demented spirit. It won't let me slow down let alone stop. I am out of control and after a quick look at my compass I run on.

I've found it, I think but of course I have not. That is nothing more than wild optimism.

Suffice to say that it took four more minutes thrashing around to get there.

I am still not convinced that the kite was on the correct boulder but my pot luck way of finding it means I have no argument to offer.

Neil got into trouble on the left hand slope route I had rejected, and lost much time by his standards and came out only seven-seconds the better.

From then on it was downhill all the way, down the slope and down the timings, for while Neil followed almost the same routes to each of the last four controls, he pulled in time at every one – except that is, and it is a very important except, the run-in to the finish.

I bettered him by twelve-seconds on that rough one hundred and fifty metre leg. You see, I told you I could run faster than him. So my ego is salved, plastered and on the mend. Maybe, of course, he just wasn't trying; he had done all his running out in the forest.

[See map and course at: http://www.routegadget.co.uk – Appendix 1; item (q)]

29

The rest of September is hectic going, on the orienteering front.

I'm not competing all the time but I am busy, busy, busy.

Perth is hosting an international sprint event, a one-off in what used to be known as the Park World Tour series.

The Tour once attracted the world's top runners to compete in complex ancient city centres across Europe for televised events which attracted big sponsorship. It went on to be used to help spread the orienteering gospel in China.

However, the sponsorship dried up. The Tour continues with occasional events when it can find backers, and while the top runners are usually out with the level of funding available, a number of world calibre competitors turn up.

So it was in Perth, where there were a dozen or so foreigners while the best of the British and other Scottish runners made up a high quality field running through the city centre streets.

World silver medallist Helena Jansson from Sweden won the women's event while Norway's Oystein Kvaal Osterbo, a regular world sprint series event winner, was best of the men.

I helped out in the press office, enjoying the action there without ever wishing that I was back full-time.

There was a junior international coming up, with Britain hosting half a dozen other European countries over two days of competition in our area. I looked over a sprint venue near their accommodation and drew up a course for them. Then I spent two days putting out control kites in another area they wanted to use for training. It is tough going physically and very technical.

Running for home on tired legs, I trip over a stone and find myself lying stretched out on the path before I know I am falling. My ribs crash down on a tree root curving just clear of the surface. It hurts and does so for a couple of weeks thereafter. I'm sure a rib is broken but since no treatment is available for such injuries I just wait for it to recover. It makes for painful running.

I spent another afternoon, ribs aching, collecting the kites.

It was all first class training, and training with the additional interest of a course to go round.

The day after the Perth event, all and sundry turned up again some thirty miles down the road at a Fife forest full of morainic hills and valleys at Devilla, near Kincardine.

One of the things about orienteering is the changes that take place in the forest.

I have run at Devilla many times and for many years but every time I am there it is different. I rarely think, "Ah. I have been here before. I remember this."

Some of the changes are man made – felling, replanting, new paths and so on. Others are natural changes which come as the trees and undergrowth mature and develop.

I can remember a time when it was a joy to run there and for some reason, despite more recent runs of a very different nature, I turn up expecting the best, only to be disappointed.

So I arrived that bright September Sunday morning full of optimism and ready for a great run.

I didn't find it.

There are no big hills at Devilla, but the going is rough and very tough.

On the way to number two the "ride" was full of thigh deep heather. I had made a detour to use it.

Coming out of two the ground was covered in the remains of heavy felled timber.

That was fairly typical. I could hardly run over much of the ground let alone fly round the course. Perfect running was well nigh impossible.

I hit every control spot on but my navigation was far from faultless.

Even if I had been running well, my perfect run ambitions were blown at number two when I took a bearing to number three from number four on the map and set out ninety degrees in the wrong direction. It took me a minute or more to see where I had gone wrong.

A few times more I wasn't careful enough, making blatantly wrong route choices the first time and the next, then failing to locate a much needed path. All three mistakes took me into avoidable tough going.

I finished just less than half way down the field.

All told it was a disastrous outing, if you'll excuse the hyperbole.

Like Devilla, Mugdock Country Park on the northern outskirts of Glasgow is a venue which goes away back in orienteering history.

I first ran there in a Glasgow League event in the 1970s. In those days we could expect a turn out of close to four or five hundred at these league events.

Large numbers of the competitors were school kids, brought in buses by teachers.

That ended in the early 1980s when local authorities tightened up on teachers' perks and found themselves with a work to rule on their hands. That lost them most of the countless hours of sport and club work teachers had been doing for nothing.

Sport in Scotland has never recovered and standards have suffered.

Results against Irish opposition in a whole number of sports highlight the effect. The two countries are similar in many ways including population size, but Ireland has had a much better international record.

Mugdock is in the upmarket Milngavie (pronounced "mul-guy") area of the city.

Glasgow has always benefited from its closeness to the great outdoors, especially on this north side.

It has a long history of walkers, climbers, mountaineers and cycling enthusiasts spilling out from all parts of the urban sprawl at weekends, many travelling by bus, to make the most of the Campsie Hills and the Highland centres beyond like Loch Lomondside and the Trossachs. Mugdock Country Park is a more recent development in this tradition.

The week after Devilla I headed there for a south of Scotland League event. It was some time since I had run in the Clobberfield sector we were about to use, so I had no great

219

hopes of remembering much about it. What I could remember was a big wet, marshy valley which runs east-west across the middle of the area, and a bit of open heath to the south of that, but as to the details needed for orienteering, these were lost in the fogs of time even with the help of an old map I pulled out of the filing cabinet in our hall.

It was raining when I got into the car with the other club runners and it was raining even more heavily when we arrived in Milngavie.

Almost miraculously it stopped as we lined up at the start.

One strange thing about running is that you can never tell before hand that you are onto a good thing. Now and again I have been feeling fine before the start, plenty of spring in my legs and no body creaks and groans to talk of, but that has not always meant a good run would follow. On the other hand, I can remember so many starts where my legs felt heavy at the start and I had no inkling that I was going to hit runners gold. I can remember an occasion lining up with "dead" legs only to find myself going into cruise mould and maintaining it over the whole course.

However, it still came as some surprise at Mugdock when I hit the hill soon after the start and found my legs still full of running.

I throttled back just to be safe, but I hit the curve towards the top breathing deeply but easily as I ran into the rough grass to find the marsh control site. Here too I felt in my element, exaggerating the "glutes" action slightly to compensate for the softer ground.

There was a big marsh too at the bottom of the steep hill on the straight line way to number three. I took one look and decided "no way" and went for the path detour.

Downhill I manoeuvred across all the protruding roots keeping the rhythm alive and so too across the bridge at the bottom and up the climb at the other side of the valley. Dropping briefly to a walk on the really steep bend, I checked the map; then back into my run I kept it going across the rocky going into the control.

I decided then that this was going to be a path run and so it was, resisting the temptation to go too fast and court anaerobic disaster, leaving enough in my legs to dodge into short stretches of woodland or heath without losing my running.

Heading back down into the big valley from twelve I momentarily toyed with taking the overland route on the long leg to thirteen but I controlled the impulse and set out on the long path detour. It paid off.

I had plenty in my legs for the short marshy section at the bottom and for the long climb on the other side. Another short walk into another steep turn again gave the chance to check the final attack on the map.

Those guys behind me were not pulling me in.

I went overland on the short, rough leg to seventeen but again my legs were fresh enough to take it; but I opted for the path run to the next despite the little climb involved and it paid off too.

With just one control and the run to the finish to go I slightly overcooked it trying to catch the teenager I had first met up with at number four.

I finished holding back a retching feeling welling up in my stomach. I had been pushing it. I breathed deeply and kept the legs jogging until it subsided.

It had been a gem of a run. Again I was competing up a level but I finished a decent fifth out of twenty-five starters, again collecting a number of fresh scalps in the process.

My navigation had been good too. I had hit most controls spot on only losing a few seconds "in the circle" at a few of them. "Sometimes I was to blame. Sometimes I wasn't. At fourteen the control description pointed towards the east end of the thicket. I went for it climbing the high bank only to find I had to dive back down the steep slope to reach the marker. My map got covered in mud as I slithered down and I had problems reading some of the detail over the leg that followed.

All of these did not detract from what had been some really spot on navigation along with some perfect running.

So was this Mugdock outing my long sought after perfect run? Had I done it at last? Was I heading home to celebrate with dinner out and a bottle of plonk? Well, no.

It had been a near thing but while it certainly rich in quality on both fronts – running and navigation there was one minor but definite mistake.

Coming out of number three I had headed for the nearby path.

Perhaps feeling a little over confident, I looked quickly at the map and decided a path side marsh would be my next attack point to go onto the little hill to the East where the fourth marker was secreted just over the summit.   Sadly I failed to notice a path junction and that the marsh came after the junction. I arrived at a path side marsh but it was one that came before the junction, one I had failed to notice on the map.

So I went in but went in too early and wasted a minute looking on the wrong hill before discovering my mistake.

Again it had been a close thing, but again I had blown it.

What a perfect run it would have been – fast, smooth, easy running, good use of the map and spot on navigation but for that one damning error.

[Devilla - see map and course at:
http://www.routegadget.co.uk – Appendix 1; item (r)
Mugdock - see map and course at:
http://www.routegadget.co.uk – Appendix 1; item (s)]

30

From time to time I meet this old guy in unexpected mirrors. It takes me some time to recognise him, to see that he is me. One thing for sure is he looks a lot younger when he has a smile on his face and is wearing his running gear.

Running doesn't just keep you fit it helps to keep you young, young in spirit more than in body, but at least in my own mind it is doing both.

All the same, there is no denying the facts of life. Nature will not be denied. That day, mid forties, when your vision begins to go, you are at the start of the big descent. Until now you have blamed the odd bad run on "getting old". You have joked about it, but you have never really believed it. You have been right. Most of us are probably running as well or even better than we have ever done as we go into our forties.

The best of my near perfect runs on the roads came when I was forty-three. I arrived late at the start line at Balloch on Loch Lomond side and the start gun had gone off while I was still making my way through the two hundred or so strong field as it set off on the twelve and a half mile run to Clydebank.

I was never a good road runner. Many of my current orienteering rivals probably ran the roads faster than I did. On my twenty or so training miles per week, I was just bettering sixty minutes for ten miles when running at my best.

To put this into some context, Ovett's coach Harry Wilson tells in his book something of the training schedules his world 1500m record breaking athlete undertook. His two session a day winter programme included several ten mile runs each week. The slowest of these was completed inside sixty minutes while his Monday afternoon "fast" outing was run at fifty to fifty-two minute pace.

At the same time, many club runners racing over ten miles in my day were out to break the "sixty minute barrier" and a six minute mile would put me quite far up the field in most of the big turnout events of the past twenty years.

That said I was considered a bit of a slowcoach back then. Nobody said as much, although once one opinionated nincompoop ironically called me a "real speed merchant". We were discussing pace, or at least he was, as we were changing for the twenty odd miler from Edinburgh to North Berwick. I went with his warped sense of humour, smiling weakly without conviction but avoiding confrontation. I really enjoyed it when I passed him around nineteen miles. Poor lad was having a bad day.

One man in my own club was not averse to making scathing remarks at the expense of one of our slower clubmates. "OK", I asked him, "so where's your Olympic gold?"

In short, there is usually someone faster than you are. My nincompoop friend, for example, would have found 1500m racer Ovett too hot to handle over his medium pace midweek ten let alone on a Monday.

However, that day as I climbed out of Balloch the slow start enforced by the people around me graduated into an easy, fast pace which started pulling people in and leaving them behind me.

My notorious high knee action took control churning over at a faster and faster cadence until I was cruising along faster than ever before with no sign of tiredness. I was in perfect running mode. I found myself, almost apologetically, passing people admittedly my betters.

With a mile or so to go it ended. My legs, suffering the effects of the repeated pounding on the road began to stiffen up and ache. I struggled home but finished in just over seventy-two minutes which surely meant I had gone through the ten mile marker at close to fifty-six or fifty-seven minutes. Maybe my great run came so late in life because I was no great shakes to start with. I remember one coach who claimed it took fifteen years to get the best from a runner. It was at least fifteen years before I had my Balloch run.

Maybe others like me spent their earlier running years learning the craft but make no mistake, peaking late in life does nothing to stave off what is to follow. That day you find yourself screwing up your eyes to read the telephone directory, look out - you are that downhill slope.

The menopause, male as well as female, is just around the corner. Women always have it rough with their hormone changes and even the male menopause lets men off lightly by comparison. The andropause, as it is called, is less dramatic than the hormone changes women go through but from around fifty most men show testosterone levels beginning to fall. Unfortunately, testosterone, as well as helping to build muscle, lends sparkle to muscle action.

Some authorities say that menopausal women have higher levels of male sex hormones than at any other time. It would be interesting to know if the sports women amongst them reap any benefit from this. In skiing terminology, at this age, you are negotiating a green level descent. Make the most of it. The slope will get steeper. When you hit sixty you are onto the black. Before the decade is scarcely under way, let alone out, younger people you ran with before are leaving you for dead and younger people you once left for dead are catching and passing you and leaving you trailing.

From forty onwards, some signs are obvious. Your hair, if you still have it, turns grey and thins. Your face becomes wrinkled and prune like. Face creams may disguise the fact for a while but their so called magical chemical ingredients will not save the day. Try botox or a face lift if you feel it is worth it.

The skin on your body will follow suit but at least you can hide that under your gear.

You are entering the world of the decrepit, with big ears and a big nose that drips whenever you are out in the cold, a world of big gutted men and big bottomed women.

This is the world of artificial joints, heart ops and colostomy bags, a world where tubes and cameras are pushed into every major orifice of your body in a bid to secure long term survival, a world where pharmaceuticals become a fact of life if not a way of life.

Osteoporosis and arthritis threaten as does cancer - lung, breast and prostate cancers being the big killers.

So too are heart disease and strokes.

Life it seems is stacked against you.

However, think on the bright side, this too is the world of bus and rail passes and concession tickets, and with retirement just around the corner you will have time on your hands to do all the things you have always wanted to do, great things like running every day if not twice a day. Spared major ill-health, you are living the life of the lotus eater, the only thing that can come between you and running nirvana is injury.

Going into October, my ribs still ached as a reminder of this.

So it was that as autumn passed my confidence was growing. I was looking forward to anchoring my growing consistency in technique and terrain running in a sound training programme. That I hoped would take me into the competition schedule ahead with a perfect run reasonably a certainty.

Then came my Thursday group run. It was already dark enough of an evening to make head torches a necessity.

We set out along the river, past the fishing hut where the ghillies host their fishing customers, and then up into the woods towards Murthly estate. All went well, everyone cruising along with a lively stream of chat, but after my two hour control collecting outing the previous day still in my legs I opted for missing out the climbs and dips of the "Birnam Walk" on the way home. I would keep to the A9 side of the railway.

Hitting the cycle path I foolishly opted to run the tarmac rather than the soft edge. I had been getting over confident about road running of late, forgetting my troubled past, or at least pushing it to the back of my mind. So when I felt discomfort in my right achilles I ignored it, an even more foolish decision. I finished the circuit and headed for home feeling none the worse. That came later that evening when I rose from my chair. The achilles had stiffened up and discomfort had become pain.

I have a long history of achilles trouble going all the way back to when I was in my late twenties and running in the then new style, light weight, thin soled, Japanese running shoes.

From then on the problem would come and go, sometimes in the left tendon, other times the right, with ever increasing layoffs from training to recover.

Several times running and stretching the achilles on soft ground climbs during orienteering would solve the problem.

A few weeks after my Balloch to Clydebank run my right achilles went again and I decided that my road running career was over. From then on it would be soft ground running only, both when training and competing. I kept to that with increasingly few exceptions.

I tried physio, with massage and ultrasound, and orthoses – medically designed insoles – but neither had any long term affect.

Then just before we moved to Birnam I developed swellings at the base of my right achilles where it was anchored to the heel. It made running more or less impossible. Walking became painful.

A consultant at the local hospital ruled out surgery and sent me instead to the podiatry department.

I went along with little enthusiasm, but it turned out to be the best health move I have ever made.

The podiatrist suggested I wear heel wedges in my running shoes and gave me a "boot".

The boot, made of stiff plastic is a calf high ankle brace held in place by Velcro strapping.

The podiatrist explained that in a damaged tendon most of the healing takes place at night when the foot is lying in an extended position with the achilles shortened. In the morning, standing up stretches the tendon forcefully, and tears the damaged area again. It never gets the chance to heal properly.

I wore the boot religiously for several weeks and - it worked and continued to do so anytime I was threatened by fresh achilles problems.

I wore it that night after my club run, but this time it failed to come up with its magic outcome. The tendon still hurt the following day. It needed rest and it got just that for I developed a cold that day – seemed like my November cold had come early - and I took time out.

By the Thursday the pain had gone so I joined the group run on the Hilton circuit along the north bank of the Tay and back.

Crossing the Telford Bridge the tendon was grumbling. I was road running again. I changed my gait, shuffling along, to protect it and opened out again as we crossed the park and took the path behind the cathedral.

Suddenly I felt two sharp twinges in the achilles and I knew my run was over. I dropped out, said sorry to the gang, and walked home feeling dejected. The next day it was hurting worse than the last time.

We left for London at the start of the week to visit our new granddaughter, Isla, in Isleworth. I planned to finish the fortnight with a run at an event near High Wycombe.

I didn't run that first week but I went walking along the Thames near Kew and into Richmond. The tendon stood up to it well and showed no sign of strain when I had a jog in the park on Thursday evening. On Saturday I tried a proper park run but, while running on soft grass was pain free, on paths or hard turf it was a different story. Again I ended up with more damage and pain than when the problem started two weeks before.

I opted out of the High Wycombe event.

I left London nursing another cold. My immune system seemed to be at an all time low. Some are starting to blame such unusual colds not on virus infections but on ticks, citing evidence that mild Lyme disease symptoms are not unlike those of the cold. Lyme disease, which can be severely debilitating, is caused by bacteria injected by tick bites.

I tried to keep fit with regular walks and the occasional bike ride in the days that followed.

I was aiming now for the final Scottish League run of the year on the last day of October. A short club run on the river path on the Thursday left no after affects and when we set out up the A9 on the Sunday I was feeling optimistic.

The venue was Inshriach forest near Aviemore on Speyside. The whole of this vast plantation is on ice age moraine terrain with clusters of bumps and hollows making for difficult navigation but the ground is covered with soft moss, mild heather and blaeberry and I was optimistic that my achilles would survive the outing.

I feel happy at the start, giving little thought to my tendon problem, as I try to focus on the job in hand. Relax the back muscles, breathe deeply, keep mobile with a few strides here and there across the pre-start area.

At last I am off. The course follows a double circle shape something like an old fashioned teacher's correction mark. It takes in a chequered area, probably an old forest experimental plot, with a mixture of thick, not so thick and open squares of trees.

I was out to run to format. In my mind, there was no doubt that if I kept my head I could do it.

I set off for number one, a saddle on top a high moraine about four hundred metres away. My tendon in mind, I dismiss the long detour path run on the left. Opting for the softer going, I target a close by summit forcing myself to keep on my compass bearing. Inside I feel I should be steering further to the left. On the way to the little hill, I work out that a massive depression ahead will set me up with a direct line to the control site while there is a fence about two-thirds way there which will act as a marker.

I breast the hill, pause for a moment to line my compass afresh and head for the depression. However, while I am using my compass I am still being pulled to the left, a feeling aggravated by the number of people running that way. I pull back to the right and hit a big depression and race down into it. On terrain like this I can run fast downhill.

As I try to follow the depression round to the right there is no right turn.

I get that, "Oh, no, I'm lost," feeling.

I find myself back up at plateau level fighting to go right to find the correct depression which I know must be there, while all the while drifting to the left.

Ultimately I hit another control. It makes me pause. Very often another control site can give a good relocation point. This one doesn't.

I move on and notice a large ride running downhill. I can't find one on the map but then I notice a fence down there. I line up the map, I.D. it as "my fence" and set off downhill.

The problem now is to decide where I am on the fence.

I opt for safety, head left to where it meets the original path, follow that to a good attack point at the next path junction and head in for the big hill. It is bigger than I thought it would be.

I get the control but it has cost me much extra distance – I set out on a four hundred metre leg and the run in from the path alone was two hundred metres – and much extra time – almost seven minutes judging by the split time results.

Is it yet another first control blunder or was it just a navigation adjustment?

The safe thing to do would be to admit, "No perfect run here then", jack it in and save my tendon.

However, I am running well, reasonably perfectly, with a good rhythm. That at least is fun so I go on.

The next little valley is easy, but I play it safe, using the path a mite more than I might have if number one had gone better.

Number three is in the chequer board and should be easy, but the problem is knowing where and when the chequer board starts. The edges are vague. My first stab at it is too early but another "adjustment" takes me in and I have lost little if any time because with this setup I am running confidently.

Number four, a big boulder just by the track side, is close by – or so I think. It turns out I am looking at number ten on the map and so waste time going off course to the wrong control. That's two more minutes wasted.

I can fool myself no longer. I have to admit it. This is no perfect run.

I am deluding myself too that my tendon is standing up to the strain. It is OK still and I carry on.

Five – easy – a peach; but six is a long way over amorphous going. I head for the big marsh as my attack point; surely I will hit that OK.

I do.

Six, then seven and eight are all picked up with spot on navigation and steady running. If only it had gone like this at the start. My problem that even if I take it easy to the first marker, I still don't get into the map and understand the shapes soon enough.

My legs are getting tired. I am beginning to think that with my recent lack of training and my tendon problem I should not be running up a couple of course levels. I'm biting off more than I can chew.

From seven to eight I veer out onto the road to find easier going and begin to notice the first signs of achilles trouble. Foolishly, I carry on.

Onto nine is another track run but with my achilles problem, my running is beginning to suffer now whenever I hit hard underfoot going.

From now on most of the controls have a path option and since I'm tired I feel forced to use them.

Ten is that boulder I visited by mistake in the chequer board. Again I have trouble identifying where I hit the chequers but no real problem finding the control. Then it's another track run to eleven before enjoying a short cross-country ridge run to twelve.

I should say short and easy. On the other hand, the path rather than the cross-country route to find the boulder at thirteen is the safest and fastest way in. I can run it always knowing where I am and where I am going.

Does it matter? I am not really competing anymore, I am out to survive.

The next again has a safe, fast road option worth a couple of minutes so I take it and all the time I am in pain. I try to ignore it but I know that it is too late to drop out now and that this is likely to take weeks to get better if, with my history in mind, it gets better at all.

Fifteen a depression and sixteen in the "fight" - a bit of a bingo affair - take longer than they should, then it is another even more damaging path run through seventeen and eighteen to the finish.

The last one up hill just consolidates the damage. I'm really running on one leg by now. At last it is over.

I limped back to the car. The results showed I had taken a few scalps despite my catastrophic blunder at number one, but that did little to raise my spirits. I was dreading the next day when I would be able to fully assess the damage.

When the next day came the damage was bad. The prognosis was bad. A walk the next weekend proved that this time the injury would take a long time to heal if at all. I went on trying to keep fit by biking the roads and trails but I knew that my next run was a long way off.

My running year was over.

My quest for the perfect run had ended in failure.

What a disappointment, the more so in that it had ended and been grounded by injury.

I was not willing to admit this. This was a strange injury because it did seem to mend quickly even if it didn't last. No, I was not willing to give in. I would check out the calendar and see if I could find another event to aim for, an event which might offer a last ditch hope.

With November all but over there was just one event and one chance left.

It was one of our club events which had been scheduled for some months for Black Spout Wood at Pitlochry, just twelve miles up the A9.

It would be my last chance, so even if my achilles showed no sign of recovery I had decided to give it a go. "Decided" is a stronger word than my thinking on the matter deserved and gives little regard to the ever changing arguments going on in my mind.

Put simply, I did not want to suffer another set back and find that I would be out of running for even longer than I had been to date.

However, at the same time, I had set out on my quest and set myself a year to do it.

This sporting quest had taken me all over Scotland, into England and across to Hungary. I did not want to opt out and pass over this last chance, the more so because of recent setbacks and the missed opportunities they had caused.

[Inshriach - see map and course at:
http://www.routegadget.co.uk – Appendix 1; item (t)]

Then on the Friday before the event, snow came.

An icy blast from Scandinavia had arrived bringing what seemed at first to be the normal November snow shower but this one went on and on. There were twenty centimetres lying in the garden and it was not going to disappear within a couple of days.

This decided it. I would go. In deep snow running would be more or less impossible in any case – BUT I could walk it.

Another snow fall came on the Saturday and I waited to see if the event organiser would cancel.

Grahame can boast a reputation in rock climbing and mountain walking. A few inches of snow was never going to put him off.

Pitlochry is an attractive tourist town with a stone worked town centre and an array of shops, cafés and bars plus a theatre of some repute. At the height of the summer the crowds lend a something happening atmosphere. At the same time it is never overwhelmed by the influx.

Black Spout Wood, which boasts a sixty metre waterfall where the Edradour burn plunges down one of the major crags, is on the south edge of the town.

It is tiny by orienteering standards, a diamond shape one kilometre by one and a quarter. The burn cuts across the area from east to west and, bordered by dramatic cliffs, provides major problems for any course planner, who must use a wooden bridge, high up, or the main road and paths on the western edge as crossing points.

The map is very large scale at 1:5,000 which is difficult to come to terms with. The features are less neat than they are on the ground and they come up faster. Mapper simplification has left out some of the smaller shapes that might warrant a place on a map on this scale.

The wood to the North is a mixture of deciduous trees, mainly oak while a sizeable open area is the small golf course belonging to a nearby hotel.

In the South the oak has been replaced in a couple of places by small spruce plantations.

As might be expected with the town close by, there is an extensive network of paths used by walkers, but not so many as to detract from what is very reasonable orienteering.

On Sunday morning it started to snow again and the forecast promised more.

I was in two minds again for there was every chance if this was widespread that the road could become impassable.

The showers came and went and the sky to the North was lighter so with a shovel in the boot of the car in case of emergencies I set off.

I was already dressed for the course in walking boots, gaiters and anorak. I did not want to be tempted into running which would surely happen if I went out in normal gear, and besides, it was freezing; if I was walking, I would have to keep warm.

The snow stopped me driving up into the car park but I walked up to find Grahame there reporting that two or three others were out in the woods. That meant that it would be competitive and not just a run or walk around. One of the essentials in any event included in my quest.

This was a low key event so the route had to be copied down from a master map. At one time, before digital printing came in, this was done at most events. It gives every chance of taking in the shape of the course before the event and noting the control features and their positions.

I jotted them down with the customary red biro and Grahame set me off.

Walking certainly gives plenty time to look at the map.

I follow the path checking off junctions on the way until I reach my path junction attack point. It looks rough going ahead with thicker than expected woods and many fallen trees covered deep in the snow.

I carry on up the smaller path until looking well off to the left I can see a steep slope which bends sharply to the East.

I strike out for it as fast as my walking boots, the snow and the hidden vegetation allows.

The trees around it are again thicker than expected. The land dips deeper than expected into the valley on the left but I am over it, clambering up onto the spur and into the control beyond.

Walking doesn't leave you winded, but strangely, the slow pace makes covering rough ground more difficult.

The way to two is again rougher than I expected.

I had figured on following the marsh at bottom of the slope but that idea is nailed dead at first sight of the red-brown, iron rich bog. That usually means deep mud – "Danger. Don't go this way."

I struggle along the slope instead.

Then it is on until I hit the path and take a bearing for the control site on the other side of an easily rising shoulder, and there it is.

There are no easy path routes to number three and again walking gear makes for an exhausting cross-country experience to the steep little valley.

It is on the slope running down to the smaller river which runs along the north edge of the area.

I struggle across another little burn nestling deep into the side of the hill, treacherous ground in the snow

After that, the going is a little less rough so I can open up a bit here and even run a few steps.

I do it in short time, seeing the control site ahead as I round the shoulder.

That's number three accounted for; let's go for four, a small crag far to the South, just across the wooden bridge above Black Spout Falls.

I climb the hill and cross the stream further up to avoid the steep slopes, then strike off across country again to hit the path that runs most of the way. Looking far ahead I can see two or three houses. The path runs along behind them.

A car goes by on the path. The driver looks as amazed to see me there trudging across the snowy woods as I am to see him. I could see he could get down the hill in the snow, but would he get back up?

Just as I pass behind the houses I note control nine, a little knoll, just off the path to the right. I can see the flag. It attracts my attention. That will help later on the course.

Four is easy. No problem. I can see the crag and the flag coming down to cross the bridge.

That's me over half way round with the time still under twenty-five minutes. Not bad for walking in this terrain but there is worse to come.

Five is something else again. The slope on this south side of the burn has very few crags but it is exceedingly steep and difficult to negotiate on the best of days, which this most certainly is not. The control is the furthest of a couple of boulders on an area where the slope eases out before dipping into a small valley running parallel to the river. That flat area makes the direct route enticing but there is much steep, possibly rough going before reaching it and I opt to climb the path to the top, follow it maybe two hundred metres and drop down again to the control. My attack point is a little knoll beside the path. I press on. There are fields across the fence alongside the wood. I measure the one hundred metres or so from the second bend in the fence. That takes me to a slight rise in the ground which might be the knoll but then again, it might not.

I look over the edge pause and head down. The descent is difficult and further than I have in mind but I carry on, hit the flat, look right, see nothing and turn to the left as expected. After twenty yards, there it is. There's the boulder but it is well camouflaged by a layer of snow and I'm on top of it before I see the marker.... a tricky one.

Number six, over three hundred metres away, is a little hill by the river edge and at first sight, just carrying on along the slope seems the best way, But that slope gets steeper further along and there are a number of crags and steep bankings in the way just before the hill itself.

Again I opt for safety, climb back to the path and set off at a mild jog. Despite the snow, this would be fast, downhill going if I could run, my studs would bite in and give a firm grip on this type of grassy surface and I would be able to open up. Frustration!

Again I count off the path junctions and pace the final hundred metres or so before I reach the small side valley

236

which is my attack point. I go into it and up the slope at the other side. There it is, down by the river, the hill. I can see the marker on top.

Again, the descent is quite perilous going but I slither and slip my way down and then bite in with my boots as I climb the hill and spike the control.

Across the river I can see Grahame and the kids at the start area. They give a shout and cheer me on.

Just for a moment I lose concentration and forget to check the control number but then as I turn away I see another control close by, one on another course. I turn back again and check the number, just to make doubly sure I am where I think I am. It's the right one.

This is going well, maybe too well. Could this be the day?

Control number seven is another knoll about two hundred metres to the South and back up hill. It is an easy one next to another of the paths; the only problem is how to get there.

It was tough coming down to this one. It will be even tougher getting back up. The other possibility is to carry on through the wood at the same level, past the other control I can see, and navigate my way round the steep part of the slope.

I do just that, again clambering through some difficult timber both standing and lying on the forest floor but fairly quickly I am there. Cornering the end of the slope and heading south.

I hit a path. It is the one I'd been running down earlier. I could go back until I find the junction with the path I am looking for, but I strike out through the woods instead. These are thicker conifers here, and there is little snow on the ground beneath them. It makes walking much easier and before I know it I have broken through onto the path I need, and equally quickly I reach the top of the slope and find the knoll and the control.

I'm enjoying this. Being able to read the map while I am walking is a big help.

This is the turnaround point. From now on I'm heading for home and still everything is on schedule for a mistake free outing. I almost said run. Well, it isn't. You don't have to remind me.

The flag for number eight is on the north side of a fenced pheasant breeding enclosure back up near the fields.

237

These enclosures, usually about five by five metres, are common on estate woodlands. Shooting is either a good day out or big business for many of the owners and the chicks, usually hatched artificially, are kept and fed in enclosures until they can fly. Wire fencing keeps foxes out.

The route choice is easy here. Go straight across the wood, avoiding the marsh on the right hand side, and attack from a bend in the path just fifty metres from where the flag should be. Problems might come from the marsh, if it is wetter than expected, or pushing through a couple of strips of denser plantation.

The alternate route is to follow the path round. It is maybe twice as far but it leads to a sharper path bend from which I can mount my attack. I go for it.

Some of the conifers are bent low over the path by the weight of snow.

It is not uncommon to find branches broken by their snow load, that or the really sharp frosts which can split the wood. It can make forest running or walking dangerous.

I turn left at the T-junction and count off the bends as I walk on along the path.

I reach the attack point and aim slightly to the right with my compass, pick up the fence and swing right to find the marker.

This one hasn't been used in pheasant breeding for a long time. Very little of the fence is left.

The map would benefit from an update. I have already found one or two new fences and others partly destroyed like this one.

Now it is number nine I'm after, and I know exactly where it is. I have been there before.

First it is back to the path and back to the bridge crossing.

Climbing the first hill, my back is aching.

Snow is blowing in hard from the fields on a very cold wind.

The forest is like a giant blanket. Just as it protected against the heat in Hungary, here it keeps out the wind and takes the edge from the cold.

Down in the valley and crossing the bridge and the wind has gone. I climb the other side and head for the cottages which I can again see through the trees.

There is the cottage and there is the knoll. Got it.

Number ten is probably the most difficult control on the course. It is a boulder which again will be covered with snow. On the face of it, all I have to do is head down the hill until I hit a path, then follow it to the left.

The path is a broken path so it is likely to be difficult to find in the snow. Looking at the map again I see a knoll which should stop me if I overshoot and there is a big clearing behind that which I should see through the trees. I have taken all this in walking the path to nine.

Using my compass as a rough guide, I head off at an angle down the hill, bounding slightly, tempting myself into a full blooded run.

This is great, but I remind myself, concentrate.

I hit one path but it is going off at an angle up the hill and is not on the map. I can't see "my" path. Just as I suspected it is not decipherable in the snow but I don't see the knoll either. (Later I find out that the "knoll" was the zero of the number ten I had written on the map beside the control). I begin to panic but there through the trees I can see the big clearing. I turn left and after twenty or so paces I see the bounder with the cane holding the flag just sticking out a fraction.

There's only the last control to go. I turn to run down hill forgetting for a moment that there is meant to be a path around, but I forget only for the smallest of moments.

It might be a path but it might not, but whatever it is it is I am going in the right direction.

Then I hit a major path going downhill. I'm jogging again.

A couple of roe deer leap off through the forest below me

This path leads right to a relatively easy control. I'm looking for a wooden seat. If I miss that then there is something seriously wrong with my mind as well as my orienteering.

No bother. My ageing mind may be crumbling but it can still spot the proverbial sore thumb.

Then it is back down the hill to the finish. The road is slippery after so many cars visiting the upper car park, but I manage to keep my feet, and run into the finish to dib for what is likely to be the last time this year.

Distance 3.2km. Time 62m6s. Mistakes 0.

So, given the occasional few yards off line, a couple of times turning around, and a couple of more changes of mind to suit changing circumstances, this looks like a perfect ...... well, a perfect walk I suppose.

Would it have been a perfect run if I had been fit to run?

I can't say.

Horror of horrors, I had gone around in walking boots and an anorak.

I can't hide my blushes.

Maybe walking in running studs and O-gear would have knocked five minutes off my time.

On the other hand the conditions on the day were in my favour.

Only half a dozen people turned out. We had snow but there was heavier snow elsewhere in the area that had kept people away. So I was on my own most of the way, with no one to distract me.

My navigation technique was well nigh spot on.

Other routes might have been better in places but then again they might not. I had weighed up the options and made my decisions.

I had hit every control.

In the days that followed there was still a nagging doubt in my own mind and finally I had to conclude that I had failed.

I had not had a perfect run.

The decision brought disappointment but over time that evaporated, for the quest had produced major success in other ways.

Both my navigation and running techniques had improved out of all recognition.

I could switch onto float mode on every run even when the going was rough.

Reading the map and the terrain had become next to second nature to me.

I have enjoyed travelling far and wide taking in new as well as familiar areas.

My quest gave an edge to my life, and extra purpose.

From midsummer through into October I was as fit as I have ever been.

I have had so many good runs this year both in competition and in training.

Need I say I will never forget that run in to the finish on the final day of the Hungarian Cup and I will long savour the memory of bounding effortlessly over the marsh on the penultimate day of the Lakes Five, that rainy day run at Mugdock and many more.

I have had fun, enjoyed myself immensely.

And …… the quest continues.

(Physio treatment in the new year cleared the achilles problem and despite three months without running, the author went on to complete a perfect run on his first event of the year at Hopetoun House near Edinburgh in February and then scored another at the JK in Northern Ireland only to be disqualified after his finger "chip" failed to record at one control).

Appendices

Appendix 1: RouteGadget
Appendix 2: Understanding Orienteering Maps

Appendix 1. Route Gadget
Maps showing the competition areas, courses and routes taken
by the author (and other competitors) can be followed at Route
Gadget internet website.
Where they are available details are given at the end of the
chapters involved directing you to this appendix.
Use http://www.routegadget.co.uk (permission Paul Frost)
In the right hand column – go to one of the following – Major
Events, "Show clubs using RG UK" (RGUK) or "Show clubs
with their own route gadget" (OWN) click on the heading if
necessary to show a list of clubs and other organisation.
Click on the appropriate club listed there.
A list of events will appear in another window.
Find the date and venue name given in the appendix and click
on this.
It takes a few moments for the Java supported map to appear.
Refresh if necessary.
In the right hand frame, click on courses to reveal the courses
list and click on the one given in the appendix (either a
number or colour). The course will appear on the map as a
series of lines and circles. The start is the triangle.
A list of names will appear in the side frame. Running down
the list will reveal the author's name "Bill Melville" Click on
the name and then on "show route" below.
Other competitors – e.g course winners - can be looked at too
if there is an asterisk alongside their name. Other courses from
the very simplest to the longest and most difficult can also be
reviewed.
All the routegadget maps used in this book are listed below.
The first, "a" the "ESOC Sprint Prologue" goes through the
procedure in detail,

a. ESOC Sprint Prologue: go to Show clubs using RG UK;

242

click Edinburgh Southern, OC; click on 2010-01-24 Sprint O 2010; wait for the map to appear (refresh if necessary); open course list - click on Prologue.

A course marked by circles and lines appears on the map.

The start is the triangle. Each circle is centred on the control feature.

The double circle is the finish.

At the same time as the course appears, a list of names appears (in the right hand column).

Find Bill Melville and click then click on "show route"

A line appears on the map showing the route taken by Bill Melville between the controls.

NB You can click on other names but only those with an asterisk have a route stored.

In the top right hand corner the times taken to run between each control are given in minutes and seconds.

b. ESOC Sprint Chase: as above, click on "Chase" rather than "Prologue".

c. North of England Championships: go to RG UK; find and click South Yorkshire Orienteers; click on 2010-01-31 Northern Champs, Edges and Big Moor; click on course 11. Find and click on Bill Melville .

d. Touch: go to OWN; Forth Valley; 2010-03-27 UK Cup Middle, Touch; Course - Veteran Men; Bill Melville.

e. Trossachs: go to OWN; Forth Valley; 2010-03-28 WRE SOL 1 Trossachs; Course – Green; Bill Melville.

f. Jan Kjellstrom Day 2: go to Major Events; JK; on new page, go to JK 2010 RouteGadget: All JK2010Routegadget events: JK 2010 Day 2; Course – 20; Bill Melville.

g. Jan Kjellstrom Day 3: go to Major events; JK; on new page go to JK 2010 RouteGadget: All JK 2010 RouteGadget events; JK 2010 Day 3; Course – 20; Bill Melville.

h. British Championships: go to Major Events; British Orienteering Championships: BOC 2010 website; results, routegadget; BOC 2010 Individual; Course – 20; Bill Melville.

i. Balkello: go to RG UK; Tayside; 2010-05-16 SOL3 Balkello; Course – Green; Bill Melville.

j. Scolty Hill: go to RG UK; Grampian; 2010-06-06 Scolty SOL4 Regional; Course – Blue; Bill Melville.

k. Scottish Championships Rannoch: go to OWN; Scottish Orienteering Association; 2010-05-29 Scottish Champs Individual; Course – 8; Bill Melville.

l. Culbin: go to OWN; Moravian; 2010-06-13 Culbin Regional; Course – Green; Bill Melville.

m. Sluie Woods: go to RGUK; Maroc; 2010-06-27 Sluie; Course – Blue; Bill Melville.

n. Lakes 5: go to RGUK; Manchester & District OC; and then 2010-08-22Swindale North Day 1; Course 12; Bill Melville. 2010-08-23 Tarn How Day 2; Course 12; Bill Melville. 2010-08-26 Caw Day 4; Course 12; Bill Melville. 2010-08-27 Helsington Barrows Day5; Course 12; Bill Melville.

o. White Rose: go to RGUK; EBorienteers; 2010-08-28 White Rose Day 1; Course G; Bill Melville.

p. White Rose: go to RGUK; EBorienteers; 2010-08-29 White Rose Day 2; Course G; Bill Melville.

q. Birsemore: go to RGUK;   Maroc; 2010-09-05 SOL5 Birsemore; Course - Short Blue; Bill Melville.

r. Devilla: go to OWN;   Scottish Orienteering Association; 2010-09-12 JHI SoSOL and CSC;   Course – Green 2; Bill Melville.

s. Mugdock: go to RGUK; Clydeside; 2010-09-19 SoSOL Clobberfield; Course – Blue; Bill Melville.

t. Inchriach: go to RGUK; Tinto; 2010-11-01 Tinto Twin & SOL7; Course – Short Blue; Bill Melville.

Appendix 2. Understanding Orienteering Maps
(See detailed list of features at www.maprunner.co.uk; click on map symbols to find out what they represent).

Brown shows land features. For example, contour lines drawn in brown show the shape of the terrain including hills, valleys, ridges, re-entrants (small hillside valley) and a number of point features such as a depression or knoll (small hill). Brown is also used to show tarmac roads.

Blue shows water features: streams (solid line), ditches (broken line), pools, lakes and larger streams and rivers (solid blue). Plus marshes –blue hatching (deeper) or broken hatching (shallow).

Black shows man made features such as buildings, paths (solid and broken lines), forest rides (long dashes), fences, walls and towers.
It is also used to show natural features such as crags, cliffs and boulders.

White shows open forest.

Green shows thicker vegetation (the darker it is the thicker the vegetation). Green hatching shows thicker underfoot going eg bracken or brambles.

Yellow shows open areas – pale for rough open such as moorland; bright for close cropped or arable fields.